Mastering the Case Interview

The Complete Guide to Management, Marketing,
and Strategic Consulting Case Interviews

Alexander Chernev

Kellogg School of Management
Northwestern University

Fourth Edition

Mastering the Case Interview

Fourth Edition | July 2007

ISBN-10: 0-9790039-0-3

ISBN-13: 978-0-9790039-0-5

Table of Contents

Preface

Most management, marketing, and strategic consulting interviews offer an interesting paradox: While nearly all candidates understand the importance of taking a systematic approach to business management, few apply the same systematic approach to prepare for the interview. Instead, they approach the interview process in a haphazard manner, relying primarily on their intuition to ensure a positive outcome. This approach is, in part, based on the common belief that interviews are company-specific and, hence, interview preparation should be done on a case-by-case basis. This is incorrect. While it is true that companies do employ diverse interviewing strategies, the core set of skills required for success is virtually the same across companies. Identifying these core skills will provide you with a deeper understanding of recruiters' needs and will help you develop a successful value proposition for each individual company. The goal of this book, therefore, is to outline the logic of the interview process and offer you a systematic approach to acing each individual interview.

The contents of this book are organized into two parts. The first part, *Mastering the Job Interview,* offers in-depth insights on how to develop a winning interview strategy. It outlines the basic interview principles, reveals the core skill set that most recruiters look for, and identifies strategies that you can use to master the job interview. The discussion is complemented by an extended set of illustrations and applications identifying specific strategies on how to ace the interview process. It includes explicit résumé and interview guidelines, sample questions and answers, and strategies for the personal experience interview and case analysis.

The second part of this book, *Mastering the Case Analysis,* offers a systematic approach to analyzing business problems typically presented in case interviews. The discussion of strategies to master the case interview is clear, concise, and to the point. This book does not simply offer you endless lists of case questions. Instead, it reveals the logic of case analysis and gives you a framework for solving a variety of problems commonly given in case interviews. This book is an effective learning tool that will help you master the case analysis.

Recruiting is not only a process of finding a job; it is also a process of discovering yourself. To be successful in the interview, you should not only have a good understanding of the needs of the recruiting company, you should also know yourself. Thus, recruiting is not only about the company discovering you, but also about you discovering who you are and who you want to be, both personally and professionally.

Good luck!

About the Author

Alexander Chernev is associate professor of marketing at the Kellogg School of Management, Northwestern University, where he teaches the core marketing management course to MBA students and behavioral decision theory to Ph.D. students. He holds a Ph.D. in Psychology from Sofia University and a Ph.D. in Business Administration from Duke University. Professor Chernev's research has been published in leading marketing journals, and he has received numerous teaching and research awards. He serves on the editorial boards of the top research journals and has advised many companies on issues such as strategic marketing, new product development, and customer management policies. Professor Chernev has provided career advice to numerous students, many of whom are currently working for Fortune 500 companies and others who are in the process of building their own Fortune 500 companies.

Acknowledgements

I would like to thank the Career Management Center at the Kellogg School of Management at Northwestern University for the input in writing this book. I would also like to thank the administration of the Kellogg School of Management for providing support for my research and teaching activities.

Part One

Mastering the Job Interview

The Job Interview

Your success at the interview is determined by your ability to identify a company that can best fulfill your goals and convince recruiters from that company to hire you. To achieve that, you should be able to clearly articulate your value proposition to the company and identify factors that make you the best candidate for the job. Your successful interview performance is a function of your individual characteristics – your skills, knowledge, and experience – as well as your ability to optimally market these skills, knowledge, and experience to the recruiting company.

Preparing for the interview involves three key steps: understanding what recruiters are looking for in a candidate, creating your unique value proposition, and, finally, persuading the recruiter that you fit the needs of the company. These three steps are discussed in more detail in the first chapter. The second chapter addresses some of the key issues in writing your resume. The third chapter offers a set of strategies to master the personal experience interview (also referred to as the behavioral interview). Finally, the fourth chapter offers an overview of the case interview and identifies some of the key case-interview strategies. An in-depth analysis of the conceptual issues involved in case analysis is offered in the second part of this book.

Chapter One

The Big Picture

Companies seek to hire candidates who can add value to their organization. The interviewer's goal is to identify candidates whose value proposition best fits the needs of the organization and who have the highest potential to create value for the company. Hence, your success in the interview is determined by the degree to which your value proposition fits the company's needs.

A useful approach to maximize your fit with the company involves the following three steps: (1) understand the recruiter's needs; (2) position yourself in a way that demonstrates you will add value to the company and differentiates you from the other candidates; and (3) clearly communicate your value proposition. These three steps are discussed in more detail in the following sections.

What Are Companies Looking for in a Candidate?

The goal of the interview is to ensure a fit between a candidate's relevant competencies and a company's needs. Because most of the newly hired associates are likely to work on multiple projects and be faced with a diverse set of problems, recruiters tend to seek candidates with a broad set of skills such as leadership, analytical thinking, and teamwork – skills that can be applied across diverse problems and industries. Therefore, when evaluating prospective candidates, companies tend to focus on candidates' general skills and competencies rather than on their experience related to a specific industry (e.g., pharmaceuticals, automotive, or technology). Even though industry experience is clearly beneficial, it is often viewed as a complementary asset to your core skills and competencies.

What skills do most companies seek? An in-depth analysis of companies' recruiting practices reveals that most management consulting, consumer products, and technology companies seek future management-track associates with more or less the same set of core attributes. These attributes can be classified into three categories: (1) core skills, (2) knowledge, and (3) company fit. These three sets of attributes are discussed in more detail in the following sections.

Core Skills

Core skills are the key abilities that are essential across all management functions. The core skill set includes the following eight skills:

- ○ ***Leadership.*** Leadership is the talent to take on a leadership role and is reflected in the ability to seize opportunity and take action, build a team and encourage a

5

shared vision, keep a clear focus on the ultimate goals, and show willingness to take a personal risk to achieve these goals.

o *Analytical skills.* Analytical skills reflect the capacity for strategic thinking, abstract reasoning, dealing with ambiguity, and an intuitive feel for numbers. Analytical skills are typically evaluated on two key dimensions: logical reasoning and quantitative skills.

o *Creativity.* In an interview context, creativity refers to the ability to come up with an original approach that offers a simple solution to a complex problem.

o *Teamwork.* Teamwork skills reflect the ability to collaborate with other team-mates, both within and across functions (e.g., within marketing and with finance, operations, and accounting).

o *Communication skills.* Communication skills reflect the ability to express ideas clearly, accurately, and succinctly, and to effectively disseminate information. Communication skills include the following abilities: listening, public speaking, writing, discussing, negotiating, and networking.

o *Management skills.* Management skills reflect your professional poise, as well as the ability to meet deadlines, manage multiple tasks, coordinate different projects, and perform under pressure.

o *Capacity to learn.* Capacity to learn reflects the ability to improve one's performance and acquire new skills.

o *Drive.* Drive refers to personal motivation for achievement, energy level, and perseverance. It reflects willingness to overcome barriers and go outside the comfort zone in order to achieve the set goals.

Companies vary in the degree to which they value the importance of the above skills. Some companies place emphasis on a subset of these skills and seek candidates who excel only on some of these dimensions (provided, of course, that they have no deficiencies on the other dimensions). In addition, different companies use different labels for the same underlying skill (e.g., innovation instead of creativity, collaboration instead of teamwork, and motivation instead of drive). Note, however, that even though companies differ in terms of the relative importance of the required skills, as well as in terms of the specific labels used to refer to these skills, the underlying skill set is essentially the same across all companies.

To illustrate, one of the key skills sought by Procter & Gamble in its recruiting efforts is the *ability to leverage resources*, which encompasses three key skills: leadership, innovation, and collaboration. In this context, leveraging resources translates to your ability to lead the company's innovation (creativity) efforts by collaborating (teamwork) with different stakeholders such as research teams, ad agencies, product development teams, and operation teams.

In the area of management consulting, McKinsey & Company is looking for candidates who demonstrate capabilities in four critical areas: problem solving (analytical skills + creativity), achieving (management skills + drive), personal impact (teamwork + communication skills), and leadership. Rather than focusing on one particular skill, McKinsey seeks well-rounded individuals with outstanding potential in each of these areas.

Knowledge

Recruiters are also often interested in your knowledge in specific areas of importance to the interviewing company. The types of knowledge most recruiters are looking for can be organized into three general categories: functional knowledge, industry knowledge, and global knowledge.

o *Functional knowledge* reflects your familiarity with a particular functional area (e.g., marketing, accounting, finance, and consulting). Functional knowledge involves understanding the basic business terminology, principles, frameworks, and theories that are essential for performing a given business function.

o *Industry knowledge* refers to your familiarity with the specifics of the industry that is of interest to the recruiting company. Industry knowledge involves understanding industry trends, the core competencies and strategic assets of the key players, as well as the dynamics of the competition and power structure.

o *Global knowledge* refers to your familiarity with the specifics of doing business in a particular country and/or geographic area. Global knowledge involves language skills, familiarity with a country-specific culture, politics, and legal system, and, on rare occasions, even connections with local government officials, business leaders, and celebrities.

Company Fit

In addition to the basic functional skills, recruiters look for certain individual characteristics that will ensure a better fit between you and the company. Factors that are likely to ensure your fit with the company can be organized into three general categories: personality fit, commitment to the company, and interest in the functional area.

o *Personality fit.* Personality fit reflects various aspects of your personality in relation to the company's culture (e.g., Would you be able to adapt easily to the company culture? Are you fun to work with?).

o *Commitment to the company.* Commitment reflects the degree to which you are really interested in the company. Needless to say, recruiters prefer candidates who have a sincere interest in their company.

o *Interest in the functional area.* This factor refers to your interest in the particular functional area involved (marketing, consulting, general management, research, etc.) The underlying assumption is that the greater the fit between your interests and the job requirements, the greater the likelihood that you will make a valuable contribution to the company.

Creating Your Value Proposition

Once recruiters' needs have been identified, the next step is to articulate your value proposition vis-à-vis these needs. The goal is to identify a corresponding skill that you can bring to the company for each of the key skills sought by recruiters. A four-step approach to articulating your value proposition is shown in Figure 1 and discussed in more detail below.

Figure 1. Creating Your Value Proposition

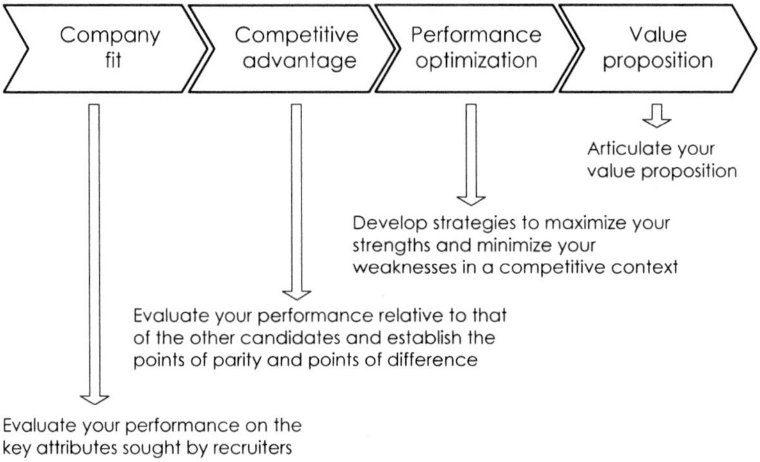

The first step is to evaluate your performance on the key attributes sought by recruiters. One simple strategy to accomplish this is to rank your performance on each attribute on a five-point scale (e.g., exceptional, above average, average, below average, poor). This will help identify areas in which you fit the company's needs, as well as areas in which you have to improve. In general, you should strive to improve in areas in which your performance is below average (or poor), as well as in areas highly valued by the company in which your performance is merely average.

The next step is to benchmark your performance relative to that of other candidates and establish the points of parity and points of difference. Because you will be compared to other candidates, it is not sufficient to be just *good*: You have to be *better* than the other candidates. One simple benchmarking method is to identify areas in which you are readily differentiated from other candidates (points of differences) and areas in which you are likely to blend in (points of parity). You can use the same five-point scale (e.g., exceptional, above average, average, below average, poor) as in the first step, but in this case your reference point is the performance of the other candidates rather than the needs of the company.

The next step is to develop strategies to optimize your performance by maximizing your strengths and minimizing your weaknesses. This is an important step, often overlooked by candidates and career counselors alike. Beware of hiding your weaknesses during the interview; this is only a temporary solution that might eventually backfire if you are not able to perform up to the standards of the company. The goal here is to improve your performance on the key attributes sought by recruiters, as well as to convert points of parity on the key attributes into points of difference. To illustrate, if you are aware that a given company emphasizes teamwork and your performance on that attribute is similar to that of the other candidates, you should consider working on improving your teamwork skills to develop a distinct advantage.

The final step is to articulate your value proposition and develop a positioning strategy. Positioning is derived by highlighting one or two aspects of your overall value proposition that most clearly communicate your value to the company and differentiate you from the other candidates. Therefore, successful positioning requires you to clearly demonstrate that your value proposition offers a better fit with the company's needs than those of the other candidates. A summary of the process of articulating your value proposition is given in the worksheet shown in Table 1.

Table 1: Positioning Worksheet

Value Proposition	Importance to the company (1=low, 5=high)	Your performance (1=low, 5=high)	Your relative performance (1=low, 5=high)
Core skills			
Leadership			
Analytical skills			
Creativity			
Teamwork			
Communication skills			
Management skills			
Capacity to learn			
Drive			
Knowledge			
Functional knowledge			
Industry knowledge			
Global knowledge			
Company fit			
Personality fit			
Commitment to the company			
Interest in the functional area			

Your unique value proposition:

Communicating Your Value Proposition

Once you understand the key value drivers for the company and articulate your unique value proposition, the next step is to develop a strategy to communicate your value proposition to the recruiting company. Communicating your value proposition starts with your résumé. The actual interview consists of several parts. It starts with an introduction, followed by questions about your personal experience and often by a case analysis. Typically, you will have an opportunity to ask questions about the company. The interview usually concludes with a closure in which you will sum up the reasons the company should hire you and establish a follow-up procedure (Figure 2). Each of these interview components is discussed in more detail below.

Figure 2. Communicating Your Value Proposition

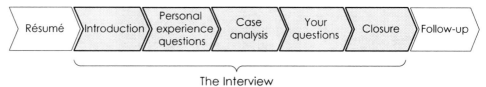

The Interview

Your Résumé

The "perfect" résumé is the one that most clearly communicates your unique value proposition to the interviewing company. Your résumé should differentiate you from the other candidates; it should underscore your value proposition and reflect your unique experience. Do not try to emulate someone else's résumé; instead, try to communicate your own story and your own value proposition.

Contrary to popular belief, your résumé is not about what you have done in the past. It is about what you can do for the company in the future. Avoid including in your résumé facts and/or details that do not enhance your overall value to the company. Each statement on your résumé should serve the purpose of communicating to the interviewer your value proposition, thus moving a step closer to eliciting an offer. For each experience on your résumé, have a short example that demonstrates the skills important to the interviewing company (see the storyboard approach and the skills-in-context matrix in the following sections). An overview of the key résumé-writing principles is given in Chapter 2.

Introduction

Most interviews begin with an introduction in which you and the interviewer greet one another and exchange a few ice-breaking comments. It is also common for the interviewer to offer a beverage. The interview is then commonly initiated with an open-ended general question of the "tell-me-about-yourself" type – a question that also serves as the transition to the personal experience portion of the interview. Because the tell-me-about-yourself question is a quite common interview approach, it is important to master a few introductory phrases so you can start the interview by positioning yourself in a way that underscores your value to the company and differentiates you from the other candidates.

Personal Experience Interview

The personal experience interview (also referred to as a behavioral interview) aims to reveal candidates' core skills, knowledge, and their fit with the company. This part of the interview usually involves asking you to provide examples of a situation in which you demonstrated the set of skills that are important to the recruiting company. The nature of the personal experience interview and strategies for mastering it are discussed in more detail in Chapter 3 of this book.

Case Analysis

Case analysis is an integral part of many consulting, management, and marketing interviews. Case questions ask you to analyze a business problem, and your insights into the case are used to help evaluate your skills, knowledge, and fit with the company. An overview of the key issues in case analysis is offered in Chapter 4, followed by a more detailed discussion in the second part of this book.

Your Questions

At the end of the interview most recruiters let you ask questions. The purpose of these questions is twofold. First, they aim to provide you with additional information about the company, its current projects, culture, and work environment. Second, the questions you ask are also a part of the interview. They are used to evaluate your interest in the company, your goals, priorities, and value system.

Be prepared to ask questions about the company, its vision for the future, defining characteristics, working environment, the company's current projects, the role that newly hired associates are likely to play, prospects for growth within the company, and the likely career track. Do not ask generic questions or those for which answers could easily be found in company literature. Instead, ask questions that will help you determine if you are a good match for the position and vice versa.

Closure

Closing the interview gives you the opportunity to summarize your unique skills and reiterate your interest in the company. You can also ask whether you can provide the interviewer with any additional information and gather insights about the next step in the process (e.g., the hiring decision process and timeframe). In addition, you can ask how to contact the interviewer to follow up on the interview (e.g., by mail, email, or phone). Keep in mind that there are many ways to close the interview; your closing should fit your personality and the interviewing style of the recruiting company.

Sometimes recruiters provide you with the opportunity to close the interview by asking you a concluding question of the type "Is there anything you would like to add (anything else we should know about you)"? You can answer this question the same way you would answer the question "Why should we hire you?" Describe the key assets and competencies that you bring to the firm. You can organize them around the three key factors: skills, knowledge, and fit with the company. This can serve as a natural closure of the interview.

Follow-up

Many recruiters view the post-interview follow-up as an important part of the process. As a result, even though follow-up activity does not guarantee that you will secure the position, if done well it could enhance your chances. In general, the goal of the follow-up is threefold: (1) thank the interviewer for his/her time and the opportunity to interview for the position, (2) reiterate your interest in the company and the position, and (3) reinforce your unique value proposition to the company. In this context, the follow-up can be an important component of communicating your value proposition to the company.

A common practice is to follow up on the interview within 24 hours, either with a thank-you letter or email. The course and the outcome of the interview should help you determine the best follow-up strategy, the content of your message, and the method of communicating it.

General Interview Guidelines

Following are a number of simple rules you need to follow before, during, and after the interview to maximize your chances for success.

▸ Before the Interview

o Research the industry and the company. Learn more about the company's vision, value system, management, product lines, and strategic challenges.

o Find out how the company conducts its interviews. Boston Consulting Group and McKinsey, for example, provide detailed personal interview advice and case analysis examples on their websites.

o Identify the reasons you would like to work for each and every company on your list. This is a question to which you should know the answer, not only because it is likely to come up in the interview, but also because it will help you articulate your level of interest in the company.

o Identify your value to the interviewing company. What is your value proposition, that is, what are the competencies and assets you bring to the company? How would you position yourself? What makes you more valuable than other candidates interviewing for the same position?

o Be fluent with your own résumé; anticipate the likely questions and have an answer ready.

o Be prepared to ask questions about the company, such as working environment, the role that newly hired associates are likely to play, and the potential career track.

o Practice. Do mock interviews with friends, teammates, and your school's career office; videotape your interviews and get feedback; observe others' mock interviews as well.

▸ During the Interview

o Always have your résumé with you, even if you expect the recruiter to have a copy.

o Your attire should fit the image of the company with which you are interviewing. The more formal and/or conservative the company, the more formally and conservatively you should dress, and vice versa. If in doubt, err on the side of being more formal/conservative. You should feel comfortable in your outfit (if you cannot feel comfortable in an outfit that fits the company's image, you probably should not interview with that company).

o Make good eye contact. This will help you engage the interviewer, establish rapport, and contribute to the interactivity of the interview.

o Be a good listener. Do not interrupt the interviewer when he/she is speaking. Be prepared to take notes.

o Be positive and avoid talking about the negatives. Instead, discuss what you've learned from difficult situations and how you have overcome challenges.

o Do not get personal. In most cases, it is a good idea to stay away from topics such as the interviewer's family, physical appearance, religious or political beliefs, age and ethnic background.

o Control your nervousness. Discover where your nervous energy goes (e.g., laughing, playing with your pen, tapping your fingers), and try to channel this energy into listening and responding to the interviewer's questions and comments.

o Do not ramble. Articulate your thoughts clearly and succinctly throughout the interview.

o Project confidence and be calm even if something goes "wrong" such as a ringing cell phone during the interview or mispronouncing the name of the interviewer. Do not be thrown off track by such mistakes; keep composure, recognize the mistake, apologize if appropriate, and move on with the interview.

o Monitor your body language. Crossed arms (considered to be defensive); tapping your feet, playing with your hair, fidgeting (an indication of nervousness or boredom); and lack of eye contact are commonly viewed as negative signs. In contrast, leaning forward and nodding while listening are usually viewed as positive signs.

o Avoid using clichés. Do not simply label yourself as "analytic," "creative," and "team-player" – these concepts are very generic and not very informative. Instead, identify specific instances that vividly demonstrate your particular skills. Tell your story, not a cliché. A vivid story has a greater chance of creating a positive and lasting impression that will allow the interviewer to later link your story to your name and skills.

o Avoid discussing salary during the early rounds of the interview. While the issue of compensation can be brought up by the recruiter at any point in the interview, in most cases you should not bring up this issue without an indication from the recruiter of their willingness to make you an offer.

o Most important – relax, try to be yourself and have fun during the interview. John W. Thompson, who, while in college, worked part time selling component stereo systems and later became the CEO of the software giant Symantec, when interviewing for a sales job with IBM ended up selling a stereo system to the interviewer.

▶ After the Interview

o A thank-you note (letter or email) can make a difference. Send it within a day of the interview and try to make it personal. If you send notes to more than one person from the same company, expect that the notes will be shared and try to make them sound different.

o When feasible, collect feedback on your performance and use this feedback to improve for the next interview. Think about what worked and what did not. Identify areas for improvement and get additional practice in these areas.

Chapter Two

The Résumé

The first impression you make on the recruiting company is created by your résumé. It is your résumé that gets you to the first round of interviews. Therefore, developing an impactful résumé is a key aspect of preparing for the job interview.

Overview

Writing a résumé is often confused with the process of identifying your value proposition to recruiters. This confusion stems from the fact that writing a résumé implies that you have a clearly defined positioning strategy that underscores your unique value proposition. Writing a résumé and positioning, however, are two fundamentally different activities. Positioning outlines your unique value proposition, whereas your résumé communicates your positioning to recruiters.

The key principle in developing a résumé is that it should not simply reflect your achievements to date. To ensure your success in the recruitment process, your résumé should go beyond offering a chronological list of your achievements and clearly indicate to the recruiter how these achievements enhance your potential to create value for the company. Therefore, each line on your résumé should not only offer information about a particular experience, but should give the interviewer a reason to hire you. This is the key to the successful résumé.

Structuring the Résumé

From a structural standpoint, most résumés are organized around three main categories: *education*, *work experience*, and *additional information*. These three résumé components are discussed below.

Education

The education section of your résumé provides details of graduate work and college education. It typically includes your degree subject, university, GPA, and any major distinctions (e.g., Magna cum laude), awards, and prizes that might help document your academic abilities. When describing your academic experiences, it is important to explain an accomplishment if you think the recruiter might not understand its importance (e.g., top 1% of students nationally). You might also include any significant academic accomplishments (e.g., thesis, major research projects) that you believe will enhance your value in the eyes of the recruiter.

Experience

The experience section of your résumé should list your prior employment, highlighting accomplishments that reveal the core skills for which a particular company is searching. The description of each of your accomplishments should include two components: the action you took, and the outcome of your action. To illustrate, "Led cross-functional team from marketing, research and development, operations, and finance to increase market share by 24% and profitability by 18%."

When describing your accomplishments, it is also important to ensure that each accomplishment communicates a particular skill (or set of skills) that enhances your value to the recruiter's company. To illustrate, the above example emphasizes your leadership skills (taking a leadership role), teamwork (the ability to collaborate with other teammates across functions), and management skills (successfully managing complex tasks).

When selecting how to describe your accomplishments, it is also important to ensure that you show breadth of skills, while prioritizing the skills that are crucial to the recruiting company. For example, when applying to consulting companies, underscore your analytical skills while documenting other relevant skills such as leadership, communication, and teamwork.

Additional Information

The additional information section of your résumé (which is sometimes labeled "other skills and accomplishments") should highlight any relevant experiences that demonstrate skills valued by the interviewing company, such as leadership, creativity, teamwork, management skills, and drive. To illustrate, you could include leadership positions, significant involvement in extracurricular activities, and significant accomplishments in sports. It is often useful to include the knowledge of any foreign languages and rate your fluency (e.g., basic, competent, or fluent). You could also include information about your interests and hobbies in cases when you think they reflect a particular skill and/or heighten your fit with the company.

When deciding which information to include, the key is to list only those activities that are likely to enhance your value proposition to the company, rather than list them just to make your résumé longer.

Style and Formatting

Although typically of secondary importance, stylistic and formatting issues, if not adequately implemented, can undermine the impact of your value proposition. Because your résumé is a form of business communication, in addition to summarizing your relevant experiences, it can also be viewed as an indication of your communication skills.

When writing your resume, it is important to use a style that projects an image that is consistent with your value proposition. To achieve that, consider using action verbs that project initiative (see "The Language of Action and Success" following this section).

It is also important to ensure that the résumé clearly communicates your value proposition. It is, therefore, preferable to use simple language and uncomplicated sentence structure. Avoid using professional jargon; your résumé should be impressive, yet easy to understand. Because the résumé is typically restricted to a single page, it is important to optimize the length-to-content ratio of each accomplishment. When describing your activities, be succinct, eliminate all unnecessary words, and focus on content.

In addition to using an appropriate style, it is also important to format your résumé in a way that highlights your accomplishments and at the same time is consistent with commonly accepted formatting guidelines. The overarching rule is that your résumé should be clearly laid out. Do not use creative formatting and fonts that are difficult to read; do not make the font size unreasonably small (e.g., to fit in more information). The focus should be on the content, not on visually distracting details.

The Cover Letter

A well-written cover letter can draw attention to your résumé and may mean the difference between your résumé being considered or disregarded. The cover letter should express your interest in the company and offer a brief overview of your skills and qualifications. Your letter should clearly articulate the reason(s) the company should hire you. It is, therefore, important to underscore your unique value proposition – the core skills that create value to the recruiting company – while differentiating you from the other candidates. When writing the cover letter, think from the recruiters' point of view and try to answer the question they will ask themselves when reading your letter: "Why should we hire this candidate?"

The cover letter should be brief, well-structured, and easy to read. One of the key goals of the cover letter is to motivate the recruiter to read your résumé. A typical mistake many candidates make is trying to include all of their accomplishments in the cover letter. These candidates forget that recruiters are bombarded with hundreds, often thousands, of résumés and cover letters, very few of which are read in great detail. Therefore, the goal of the cover letter is to help you break through the clutter by effectively communicating your unique value proposition. Keep your cover letter short and to the point.

The Résumé as an Introduction to the Personal Experience Interview

One of the most common mistakes in résumé writing is thinking of the résumé as a free-standing document without explicitly considering the impact of the information offered in the résumé on the course of the interview. In fact, interviewers typically rely on the information provided by your résumé to decide which questions to ask you, as well as to determine the overall course of the interview.

To increase the likelihood that you are given the option to demonstrate your value to the recruiter's company, make sure that your résumé prominently features accomplishments that you would like to discuss during the interview. Typically, these events involve accomplishments that best demonstrate the skills you possess that are most valued by recruiters. It is also important to be prepared to elaborate on each point in your résumé.

To help you better position yourself during the interview, provide a clear and understandable description of the nature of the projects with which you were involved, the actions you took, and the results you achieved. Avoid ambiguity in your résumé; do not use terminology and abbreviations that are likely to be unfamiliar to recruiters. Your goal should be to focus the interview on your ability to create value to the recruiter's company rather than spend most of the interview clarifying marginally important points.

Exhibit 1. Résumé Example: Financial Background

RICHARD BESSLER
2001 Sheridan Rd
Evanston, Illinois 60208
(847) 491-3300
rbessler@kellogg.northwestern.edu

EDUCATION

2006-present

KELLOGG SCHOOL OF MANAGEMENT   Evanston, IL
NORTHWESTERN UNIVERSITY
Candidate for Master of Business Administration degree, June 2008.
- Cumulative GPA: 4.0/4.0.
- Intended majors in Accounting and Finance.
- Goldman Sachs and Morgan Stanley Fellowship Finalist.
- Elected Investment Banking Club, Finance Club Co-Chair.
- Appointed Graduate Management Association (GMA) International Co-Chair.

1997-2001

WHARTON SCHOOL, UNIVERSTIY OF PENNSYLVANIA   New Haven, CT
Bachelor of Arts degree in Business, June 1998. Concentration in Finance.
- Dean's list, graduated cum laude.
- Associate Director, Wharton Peer Advising
- Financed 55% of education through work-study, scholarships, and loans.

EXPERIENCE

2004-2006

WACHOVIA SECURITIES   Charlotte, NC
Associate, Public Portfolio Management (Credit Capital Markets)
- Launched healthcare segment of proprietary credit portfolio consisting of over 80 pharmaceutical, biotech, medtech, medical products, and healthcare services companies, representing over $4.5 billion of debt exposure.
- Managed $1.6 billion healthcare portfolio to drive P&L by buying and selling bond, loan, convertible and credit derivative securities.
- Developed research reflecting proprietary investment opinion, industry dynamics, and company's financial and strategic profile for constituents across capital markets' internal platform.

2003-2004

BANK OF AMERICA   Chicago, IL
Analyst, Strategic Alliances & Investment (Principal Investing)
- Evaluated and executed strategic private equity investments across bank platform and provided investment, M&A, and JV strategic advisory services.
- Analyzed and directed variety of investment structures, including initial capital outlays, follow-on funding and warrant transactions.
- Supported deal process through due diligence, valuation, execution and post-transaction monitoring of investment.
- Tracked regulatory requirements and prepared investment reviews for 43 holdings representing over $150 million of invested capital.

2001-2003

GOLDMAN, SACHS & CO.   New York, NY
Analyst, Investment Banking Division (Mergers & Strategic Advisory Group)
- Advised clients on variety of M&A and financing transactions in consumer products and industrial sectors.
- Developed comprehensive valuation models, including discounted cash flow, merger, leveraged buyout, comparable-company and comparable-transaction analyses.
- Helped both public and private clients to evaluate and develop M&A, takeover defense, corporate structuring, and financing strategies.
- Prepared presentations for senior management groups, boards of directors, and investors, including pitch materials, offering memoranda, fairness opinions and road show presentations.

ADDITIONAL DATA
- Coordinator for St. Thomas's Soup Kitchen, accommodating over 300 people twice a week.
- 2003 NOVA National Mountain Bike Series winner (1st out of 430).

Exhibit 2. Résumé Example: Marketing Background

RYAN HAMILTON
2001 Sheridan Road
Evanston, IL 60208
(847) 491-3300
rhamilton@kellogg.northwestern.edu

EDUCATION

2006-present   **KELLOGG SCHOOL OF MANAGEMENT**   Evanston, IL
NORTHWESTERN UNIVERSITY
Candidate for Master of Business Administration degree, June 2008.
- Cumulative GPA: 3.8/4.0.
- Intended majors in Marketing and Organizational Behavior.
- Elected Marketing Club President, 540 members.

1996 - 2000   **BROWN UNIVERSITY**   Providence, RI
Bachelor of Arts degree in Applied Math-Economics, Bachelor of Arts in History, May 2002.
- Elected Vice President of Education and Treasurer, Brown Investment Group.
- Awarded *Wall Street Journal* Prize for top Economics student.

EXPERIENCE

2000-2006   **THE CLOROX COMPANY**   Oakland, CA
Associate Marketing Manager, Brita, 2004-2006
- Led new brand and advertising strategy development for Brita. Managed $20MM budget.
- Developed insights into new target consumer intended to redefine all marketing communication including: advertising, packaging, consumer promotions, public relations, and in-store merchandising.
- Supervised development of the integrated marketing communications plan for FY06. Managed process and ensured alignment with large cross-functional team, as well as senior management.
- Developed new Brita Hispanic TV commercial ($4MM) and general market Print campaign ($4MM).
- Managed Wal-Mart operations team to influence priorities at Wal-Mart. Led defensive effort to minimize impact of new low-priced competitor in the water filtration category.

Associate Marketing Manager, 409 All Purpose Cleaner, 2002-2004   Oakland, CA
- Managed the repositioning of 409 Lemon to 409 Antibacterial Kitchen, leading to sales gains of +$7MM in customer sales and distribution in an additional 2,500 Wal-Mart stores. Developed dedicated print advertising to support August 2004 launch.
- Analyzed and recommended optimal assortment by retailer, resulting in 15% growth potential.
- Managed 409 refill bottle redesign, projected to deliver $500M/yr in cost savings and enable increased distribution.
- Responsible for "wipes revitalization" plan due to poor market results after launch. Analyzed pricing rollback options to recommended elimination of one scent effective June 2004.

Marketing Associate, Tilex and Liquid Plumr, 2000-2002   Oakland, CA
- Led development of a new Liquid Plumr product with 10% sales growth potential to the franchise. Identified opportunities to conduct unconventional consumer research with a new consumer target.
- Managed cross-functional team to develop Tilex Soap Scum Remover product improvement. Guided team to develop more consumer-relevant technical testing methodology. Team successfully closed performance gap vs. competition, resulting in a consumer-preferred product, (58/42 blind win).
- Created and executed $7MM consumer promotion plan for Tilex and Liquid Plumr. Integrated promotions with overall brand positioning to deliver consumer preference at shelf. Executed $4MM defensive campaign for Tilex that grew dollar share +5 pts in one year.
- Accurately managed Liquid Plumr volume and profit ($75MM in customer sales) during a highly competitive year with three new entrants in the category.

ADDITIONAL DATA
- Fluent in Japanese.
- Finalist in 2001 Mavericks Big Wave Surf Competition (Placed 15 out of 700).
- Special Olympics Track and Field Coach.

Exhibit 3. Résumé Example: Consulting Background

JOANNE FREEMAN
2001 Sheridan Road
Evanston, IL 60208
(847) 491-3300
jfreeman@kellogg.northwestern.edu

EDUCATION

2006-present   **KELLOGG SCHOOL OF MANAGEMENT**   Evanston, IL
NORTHWESTERN UNIVERSITY
Candidate for Master of Business Administration degree, June 2008.
- Cumulative GPA: 4.0/4.0.
- Intended major in Finance.
- Winning team in 9th annual A.T. Kearney Global Prize consulting competition.

1996-2000   **DARTMOUTH COLLEGE**   Hanover, NH
Bachelor of Arts degree in Economics, June 2000.
- Graduated *magna cum laude*
- President, *The Dartmouth Review.*

EXPERIENCE

2005-2006   **ZS ASSOCIATES**   Evanston, IL
Consultant
- Designed a 5-year business strategy across Europe, Asia and the U.S. to facilitate $800MM growth through product integration, strategic account management, manufacturing cost reduction, unprofitable market exits, and increased quality focus.
- Managed a 10-person team over a 2-year period to design and execute the redeployment and market converge initiatives of a 2,000-person sales force for a $5 billion company.

2001-2005   **PRICEWATERHOUSECOOPERS**   Hopewell, VA
Senior Associate 2003-2005 (ranked top 5% of peer group)
- Consulted with top-20 Consumer Finance companies, performing multiple services that included process redesign projects, complex cash flow modeling, and operational risks and controls.
- Managed up to four internal and external staff on project-by-project basis.
- Chosen by Mortgage Bankers Association of America to present on the "Top 5 in '05" at the Mortgage Servicing Conference in Orlando, FL in front of audience of 150 people.
- Selected to lead Small Business team on a Basel II initiative at a large commercial bank.
- Presented on Mortgage Servicing Rights at Executive Enterprise, Inc.'s annual Risk Management Conference in Washington, DC.
- Selected to perform Sarbanes-Oxley review of client's entire mortgage cycle to identify and document all risks, controls, and weaknesses.

Associate 2001-2003   Hopewell, VA
- Designed significant portion of User Acceptance Testing of cash flows for $5 million initiative.
- Led analysis that identified more than $6M in annual benefits for a top-five Mortgage Bank.
- Conducted interviews with all levels of the Servicing Unit at a large Consumer Finance client, which led to the development of cash flow specifications to support a loan-level database.

2000-2001   **MARRIOTT HOTELS**   Reno, NV
Project Manager
- Performed site assessments and conducted reviews and analyses of key performance factors.
- Designed and implemented a cost control and project management program to streamline internal communication and increase information sharing around hotel construction projects.
- Developed market studies that contributed to the creation of a $400 million development plan.

ADDITIONAL DATA
- Fluent in Spanish.
- Cofounder and Chairwoman of Greensoft International Recycling, a non-profit focused on coordinating international technology refurbishing and donation efforts (2003-present).

Exhibit 4. Résumé Example: Engineering Background

BENOÎT GAILLARD
2001 Sheridan Road
Evanston, IL 60208
(847) 491-3300
bgaillard@kellogg.northwestern.edu

EDUCATION

2006-Present   **KELLOGG SCHOOL OF MANAGEMENT**   Evanston, IL
NORTHWESTERN UNIVERSITY
Candidate for Master of Business Administration degree, June 2008.
- Cumulative GPA: 3.9/4.0.
- Intended majors in Management & Strategy.
- Winner of 10th annual Carnegie Mellon Operations Management Competition.

1992-1997   **CAMBRIDGE UNIVERSITY**   Cambridge, England
Master of Engineering degree in Chemical Engineering, June 1997.
- Awarded University Prize for Research Project: "Light Emitting Diodes" (ranked first of 120).
- Elected President, Chemical Engineering Society.

Bachelor of Arts degree in Chemical Engineering, June 1996.
- Awarded University Prize for Design Project: "Ethanol Recovery " (ranked first of 65).
- Awarded Junior and Senior Scholarships (1st class Honors exam performance).

EXPERIENCE

2003-2006   **MERCK & COMPANY, INCORPORATED**   Hertfordshire, England
Senior Engineer, Pharmaceutical Process Technology, 2004-2006
- Directed a cross-functional team to technically assess outsourcing options for a critical material to capture a five-fold reduction in material costs for a pharmaceutical product.
- Designed and led execution of an intra-site manufacturing process transfer in Australia that reduced annual discards for a product by more than $1MM.
- Provided equipment, process, productivity, and troubleshooting support to 9 manufacturing sites worldwide for 7 product families, generating more than $4 billion in annual sales.
- Spearheaded an operational excellence initiative and led cross-functional team to streamline the use of statistical control for monitoring manufacturing process, reducing discards globally by 9%.

Lead Technical Engineer, Pharmaceutical Process Technology, 2003-2004
- Designed the transfer of a new manufacturing process to a Japanese site to support the positioning of a $2 billion/year pharmaceutical product for sale in Japan.
- Coordinated and executed pilot scale development work for 2 new pharmaceutical products and served as the functional representative on cross-divisional drug development teams.
- Reduced discards due to quality defects for a $2.4 billion product manufactured at 4 sites by creating a process database and proactively monitoring the data.

1999-2003   **EXXON**   Surrey, England
Lead Technical Engineer, 2001-2003
- Managed multiple project teams in developing a state-of-the-art, multimillion dollar semiconductor tester, by facilitating collaboration, as well as providing technical guidance.
- Led a 10-person team to initiate and execute projects to address a strategic gap, which led to $20 million in additional revenue.
- Primary contact in R&D to aid customer and marketing teams in new business development.

Senior Development Engineer, 1999-2001
- Created innovative approaches to the testing area, leading to the commitment of more than $120 million in revenue from our top target customers.
- Consulted with customer teams to resolve technical defects and assess customer needs.

ADDITIONAL DATA
- Fluent French and English, conversational Spanish and German.
- Authorized to work in U.S.

The Language of Action and Success

Your résumé should project a winning management style; it calls for using active language to effectively communicate your unique value to the company. A number of common action phrases used in résumé writing and during the interview to communicate your achievements are given below:

o   Accelerated [performance, development, customer acquisition]

o   Accomplished [project, goal, task]

o   Achieved a goal

o   Administered [contract, project, task]

o   Aligned [people to a goal, goal and strategy, strategy and tactics]

o   Analyzed [financial impact, organizational fit, data]

o   Assessed [risk, impact, competitive threat, market forces]

o   Assisted [senior management, clients]

o   Awarded [scholarship, grant, prize]

o   Bridged a gap

o   Capitalized on an opportunity

o   Collected [market data, competitive intelligence]

o   Completed the project [on schedule, under budget]

o   Conceived [idea, strategy, project]

o   Conducted [financial, marketing, competitive, sensitivity] analysis

o   Coordinated communications to internal and external [constituencies, stakeholders, entities]

o   Coordinated team efforts

o   Created [a vision, strategy]

o   Defined [scope, strategy, implementation plan]

o   Designed [strategy, tactics, implementation plan]

o   Developed [strategy, marketing plan, vision]

o   Devised [program, strategy, project]

o   Directed [project, employees, program]

o   Established [guidelines, benchmarks, goals]

o   Estimated [market potential, competitive response]

- Evaluated new business opportunities
- Evaluated market reaction to [promotions, advertising, price]
- Exceeded a goal
- Executed [strategy, business plan]
- Expanded [operation, project, scope]
- Facilitated [process, acquisition, implementation]
- Formulated [hypotheses, strategy, action plan]
- Fostered collaboration
- Generated [new approach, solutions]
- Identified [strategic gap, opportunities, alternatives, strategies]
- Implemented [program, strategy, goals]
- Improved [communications, customer satisfaction, morale, performance]
- Increased [profits, revenues, sales volume]
- Initiated [project, activity, policy]
- Interacted with [clients, project management, stakeholders]
- Led [product management team, cross-functional teams]
- Managed [project/cross-functional team, the development and implementation of a strategic plan]
- Modified [program, strategy]
- Motivated [team, employees, stakeholders]
- Negotiated [deal, settlement, acquisition]
- Optimized [business model, resource allocation policy, operating structure]
- Outlined [strategy, vision, project]
- Persuaded [clients, management]
- Planned [mergers, strategies, projects]
- Prepared [client reports, presentations]
- Presented [analysis, recommendations, solutions]
- Produced [results, projects, goals]
- Rebuilt [infrastructure, confidence, strategies]
- Reduced [costs, exposure, vulnerability, response time, turnaround time, turnover, uncertainty]
- Resolved a conflict

- Responded to a crisis
- Responsible for [new product development, strategic planning, customer management, project, team, new client development, client account]
- Set [goals, policy]
- Solved a problem
- Streamlined [process, operations, policy]
- Strengthened [reputation, performance]
- Structured [new venture, deal]
- Surpassed [requirements, goals, projections]
- Took [a risk, initiative]
- Won [award, contract, competition]

Chapter Three

The Personal Experience Interview

Overview

The personal experience part of the interview (also referred to as the "behavioral" or "informational" interview) is about getting to know you. There is no fixed format or agenda. This part of the interview usually involves asking you to provide an example of a situation in which you have demonstrated a particular skill (e.g., leadership, analytical, etc.). These questions often begin with "tell me about a time when ..." or "give me an example of...." The goal is to let you demonstrate mastery of the key skills by recounting a relevant story from past experience.

A frequent mistake made by candidates is using general skill descriptors such as "analytic," "creative," and "leadership." It is not uncommon to hear a candidate claiming to be "a natural leader and team player, with analytic and problem-solving skills." As a result, interviewers are likely to hear the same answers repeatedly. This is because most candidates use the same strategy to prepare for interviews: They identify their competencies and attributes, research the industry, company, and job description, and rehearse guidebook answers to typical questions. Therefore, it is important to think from the point of the interviewer, who is faced with a number of candidates, all claiming to have leadership, analytical, and communication skills, to be team players, and to provide the perfect fit for the interviewer's company.

The problem with simply labeling yourself as "analytic," "creative," and "strategic" is twofold. First, these are very general concepts and, as such, they lack specific meaning. Simply stating that you "have analytical skills" does not communicate any relevant information to the interviewer (except that you have figured out that being "analytic" is important). The interviewer cannot even be sure that you actually understand what being "analytic" means. What the interviewer is looking for is a story that reveals a particular skill.

The second concern with using general skill descriptors such as "analytic," "creative," and "strategic" is that recruiting is not just a process of evaluating each candidate but is a *choice* among candidates. Your goal is not only to convince the interviewer that you fit the position requirements but also that you are the *best* among all candidates. Hence, you need to differentiate yourself. Simply saying that you are "analytic," "creative," and a "team player" will not differentiate you, because a great number of other candidates will be rehearsing exactly the same phrases and claiming the same attributes.

A successful interview communicates your value proposition in a meaningful and memorable way that will establish your superiority over the other candidates.

This can best be achieved by describing specific instances that vividly demonstrate your particular skills. Tell *your* story, not a textbook example. Your story should be specific and demonstrate your skills in a particular context. Make your story colorful and expressive, which will make it stand out and be more memorable. The interviewer is more likely to relate to a vivid story, and will probably pay closer attention and become more involved in the interview when the story is engaging. The story you tell presents an opportunity to create a positive and lasting impression that will allow the interviewer to later link your story to your name and skills.

Think of the interview as an opportunity to communicate your value proposition while differentiating yourself from other candidates. The interview is a marketing communication task in which you must convince the interviewer that you can satisfy his/her company's needs better than the other candidates. One rarely sees an ad in which a company simply claims product superiority. Instead, a good ad tells you a story that demonstrates the product's benefits in a specific context. You should do the same. The storyboard approach discussed in the following sections shows you how to achieve that.

The Introduction Question

The interview typically starts with an introduction question asking you to offer an overview of who you are, of your career achievements, and/or of your life so far. The prototypical introduction question is "Tell me about yourself." This question is so common that not having a ready answer is inexcusable. Yet, many candidates come to interviews without a prepared answer and instead try to make up an answer on the spot. Even among those who do have a ready answer, many give a textbook cliché introduction, thus failing to take advantage of the opportunity afforded by this question to articulate their value proposition and differentiate themselves from the other candidates. Therefore, it is crucial not only to have a ready introduction, but also to have an introduction that will give you an edge over the other candidates and will bring you closer to receiving an offer.

A useful approach to developing a meaningful introduction is to structure your answer around four key elements: introduction, accomplishments, skills, and value. These four elements, illustrated in Figure 1, can be summarized as follows:

o Start with a brief introduction summarizing your most important and/or most distinct characteristics.

o Briefly summarize your key *accomplishments* to give the interviewer a better picture of what you have achieved so far in your professional career.

o Highlight key *skills* and competencies you have accumulated so far.

o Articulate your *value* to the recruiter's company by linking your skills and accomplishments to your ability to create value for the company better than any of the other candidates.

Figure 1. Structuring Your Introduction Statement

When preparing for the introduction question, keep in mind that your answer not only gives you the option to articulate your value proposition to the company early on in the interview; it also gives you the option to change the course of the interview by focusing the interviewer's attention on the accomplishments, skills, and value highlighted in your answer. Indeed, it is often the case that issues brought up by candidates in the introduction become the focal points of the interview.

It is also important to keep in mind that in most cases you will not be able to control the pace of the interview; instead you will have to follow the pace set by the interviewer. This implies that you should have several versions of your introduction: a brief version and a few extended ones. However, given that this is an introduction, even the most detailed version of your answer still needs to be short and to the point.

The Storyboard Approach

The storyboard approach introduced here is based on the relatively simple idea of telling vivid and detailed stories to communicate your skills in a specific context. Instead of simply claiming that you have "analytical skills," tell a story that demonstrates how you applied these skills to solve a specific problem. Not only is this more likely to convince the interviewer that you actually have the skill, it will also make you more distinct and your story more memorable.

To make your story engaging, informative, and impactful, you can use the following three-step format, illustrated in Figure 2:

o Start by describing the decision *context* and the problem that you were trying to solve.

o Next, describe how you approached the problem and what *actions* you took. Be specific and identify how you were able to solve the problem, what strategy you employed, and how you carried out this strategy. Make sure to underscore how you personally made a difference.

o Finally, describe the *results*. Quantify the outcome, if possible, and be sure to explain what qualifies that outcome as a success.

Figure 2. The Storyboard Approach to the Personal Experience Interview

The key element in the **context-action-results** (C-A-R) approach is the action step, which often is the focal point of the story. A useful format for presenting a

problem-driven action involves the following approach. Start by summarizing what you did to solve the problem and then, time permitting, elaborate on the specific steps describing your action. These include: (1) identifying the problem, (2) generating several possible solution scenarios, (3) gathering additional information, (4) soliciting input from others, (5) selecting the best alternative, (6) designing a plan to implement the proposed solution in a timely manner, and (7) evaluating the results to learn from the experience.

In addition to the context-action-results model, another conceptually similar approach is the **situation-task-action-results**, or S-T-A-R model. Here situation refers to the problem at hand and task refers to your assignment – what you were asked to do or, in cases where you initiated the action, how you interpreted the situation and formulated the task. As can be seen from Figure 3, both the C-A-R and S-T-A-R approaches are essentially identical. Some prefer the C-A-R approach because it is simple and more intuitive. Others prefer to use the S-T-A-R approach because it sounds more relevant to a candidate's situation: Everyone wants to be a "star" in the job market. Ultimately, the choice between the C-A-R and the S-T-A-R approach is arbitrary; use whichever one is more comfortable for you.

Figure 3. C-A-R and S-T-A-R Storyboard Frameworks

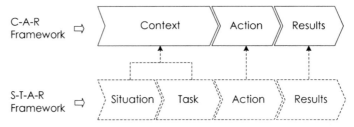

The Skills-in-Context Matrix

The storyboard approach is very useful for illustrating a specific skill (e.g., leadership) in a particular context (e.g., prior job). There are, however, multiple skills that are of interest to interviewers. There are also multiple contexts in which these skills can be shown: prior work experience, prior academic experience, various extracurricular activities, etc. Therefore, it is important to have a system for navigating through different skills in different contexts during the interview. This system is the skills-in-context matrix.

The skills-in-context matrix cross-tabulates the key skills and the different contexts in which these skills can be demonstrated. An illustration of the skills-in-context matrix is shown in Figure 4. The skills factor of the matrix comprises the eight key skills identified in the previous section: leadership, analytical skills, creativity, teamwork, communication skills, management skills, capacity to learn, and drive. The context factor, on the other hand, is represented by the different experiences that provide an environment in which some or all of the above skills might be exhibited.

Figure 4. The Skills-in-Context Matrix

	Context 1	Context 2	Context 3	Context 4
Leadership	C-A-R	C-A-R	C-A-R	C-A-R
Analytical skills	C-A-R	C-A-R	C-A-R	C-A-R
Creativity	C-A-R	C-A-R	C-A-R	C-A-R
Teamwork	C-A-R	C-A-R	C-A-R	C-A-R
Communication skills	C-A-R	C-A-R	C-A-R	C-A-R
Management skills	C-A-R	C-A-R	C-A-R	C-A-R
Capacity to learn	C-A-R	C-A-R	C-A-R	C-A-R
Drive	C-A-R	C-A-R	C-A-R	C-A-R

For MBA students, the usual contexts are their college experience, prior job experience(s), MBA program experience (team projects, club involvement, etc.), as well as various extracurricular activities (sports, volunteer work, hobbies, etc.). Some of the contexts, such as prior job experience and academic experience, are typical for all candidates. Others are more specific, and it is up to you to introduce that context during the interview (either in the conversation or by featuring it in the résumé).

A common mistake made by candidates is the lack of a systematic approach to linking specific skills to specific contexts (e.g., analytic skills in college, leadership in prior job, teamwork during the MBA program). As a result, candidates are often unprepared to address interviewers' questions about a specific skill in a particular context (e.g., "tell me about your leadership skills at your most recent job"). To help you avoid making this mistake, the skills-in-context approach calls for a story that demonstrates *each* of the key skills in *each* of the contexts implied by your background. Thus, when asked about a specific skill (e.g., leadership), you will be prepared to tell a story demonstrating this skill across different contexts (skill-based stories). When asked about a specific context (e.g., prior work experience) you have readily available stories that demonstrate your relevant skill set (context-based stories). You will also have a story ready when asked to discuss a specific skill (e.g., leadership) in a particular context (e.g., prior job).

To illustrate, imagine that you have held two jobs prior to enrolling in an MBA program. The natural contexts in which your skills could have been demonstrated are (1) college experience, (2) job #1, (3) job #2, and (4) current MBA experience. To be prepared for the interview, you should be ready to discuss each of the eight key skills in each of the above four contexts. In particular, you should be ready to answer questions about each skill across different contexts as well as questions about different skills demonstrated in a particular context (Figure 5). You should also be able to discuss a particular skill in a specific context. To illustrate, if you are asked to talk about your leadership skills at job #2, you should have a ready story that describes the company context, the action taken, and the results (Figure 6).

Figure 5. Using the Skills-in-Context Matrix to Answer Skill-Based and Context-Based Questions

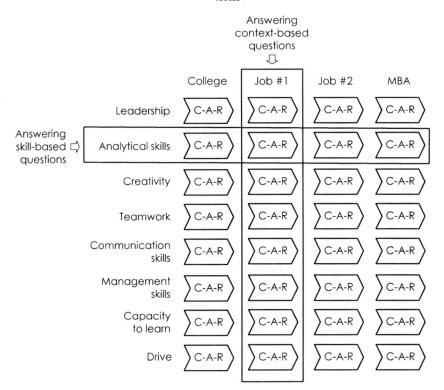

Figure 6. Using the Skills-in-Context Matrix to Answer a Question about a Specific Skill in a Particular Context

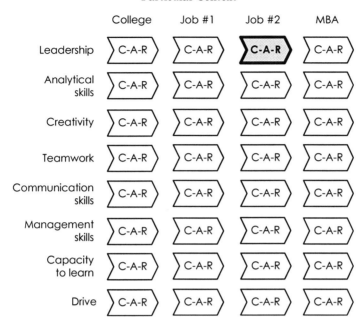

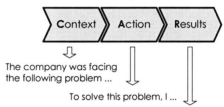

The skills-in-context approach requires a substantial amount of thinking on your part. In many cases it is difficult to come up with examples of different skills in all contexts. Yet, articulating specific instances that demonstrate each relevant skill in different contexts can go a long way to ensure that you have effectively communicated your value proposition to the interviewer.

Typical Opening Questions and Answer Strategies

Most interviews begin with an open-ended general question designed to break the ice and set the tone for the interview. The introduction question also gives candidates an opportunity to state their value proposition early in the interview. Answer strategies to some of the most common introduction questions are given below.

o Tell us about yourself.

This is the prototypical question to start the interview. Prepare a narrative that highlights who you are and, most important, your unique value proposition to the interviewing company. You cannot avoid this question and should have a ready answer for it. In fact, even if not asked, you should still work the answer into the interview (e.g., "it might be helpful if I start by providing my background"). Prepare a one-, three-, and five-minute version of your story so that you have the option to choose the narrative that best fits the interview timeframe.

o Walk me through your résumé and explain the decisions you have made to date (Variation of this question: Describe your career progression to date).

This is a straightforward question and you should be able to answer it in about two minutes, but be prepared to go into much greater depth, if asked. As you walk the interviewer through your résumé, make sure to use your accomplishments to underscore your value proposition to the company (i.e., why the company should hire you).

o Why would you like to work for us?

You should have an answer for this question. If you can't answer it, you should take this company off your list.

o Why should we hire you?

Offer a brief summary of your value proposition. Describe the key assets and competencies that you bring to the firm. You can organize them around the three key factors: skills, knowledge, and fit with the company.

o Why did you decide to get an MBA, and why did you choose to do it at this school?

Your answer should focus on your ambitions to grow professionally. Explain why the school you have chosen to attend is the best fit for you given your current skills and long-term goals.

Questions Testing Your Core Skills

The eight basic core skills for which companies are looking are: leadership, analytical skills, creativity, teamwork, communication, management, capacity to learn, and drive. Examples of common interview questions for each of these skills are given below.

▸ Leadership

○ Give an example of your ability to build motivation in your co-workers, classmates, or a volunteer committee.

○ What leadership roles have you played prior to applying for a position with our company?

○ Have you ever had an idea or a goal to achieve something that required action by other people? How did you implement this idea?

○ Describe a situation in which you led a group to complete a complex assignment and motivated others to get the work done on time.

○ How would you build a team from independent individuals?

○ How do you motivate people?

○ How do you help ensure that your team meets project deadlines?

○ Describe a situation demonstrating your ability to foster teamwork early on and prove that you have the potential to become a team leader.

○ How did you foster effective and open communication and achieve your and your teammates' goals?

○ How did you build a shared vision and shared goals?

○ How did you resolve differences of opinion and group tensions?

○ How did you instill in others an atmosphere of support, responsiveness, and respect?

○ Describe a situation in which you were in charge of a group of people and moved something forward. How did you mobilize the team to work toward achieving the result you chose?

▸ Analytical Skills

○ Tell me about your analytical skills.

○ You seem to have strong analytical skills. Why do you believe you can handle the requirements of the job you are applying for?

○ Tell me about a complex problem you had to solve, and walk me through your thinking as you solved it.

- Describe a situation in which you took a complex problem and designed an actionable strategy to solve this problem.
- Describe a situation in which you had to make an important decision without having all the necessary information at hand.
- How would you describe your approach to solving problems?
- Describe a situation in which you had to apply your skills to learn a new technology or a process.

▸ Creativity

- In your work experience, what have you done that you consider truly creative?
- How would you define creativity?
- Would your friends/colleagues describe you as a creative person?
- Tell me about a creative solution that you developed for a difficult problem.
- Describe a situation in which you developed a unique and resourceful solution to a difficult problem.
- Describe a situation that demonstrates your ability to see multiple options or look at things from a different point of view.
- Which of your creative accomplishments has given you the most satisfaction?

▸ Teamwork

- How would your team members describe you?
- Describe a recent unpopular decision you made and the results of this decision.
- Do you prefer to work by yourself or with others?
- What makes for a good team member?
- What types of people do you have trouble getting along with?
- What was the most challenging group you successfully worked with?
- How do you determine the role you play on the team?
- Tell me three positive and three negative things your team members would say about your interactions with them.
- What is the most difficult thing for you in working with your team members?
- What makes you most effective with people? What kinds of people do you find most challenging? What conflicts or difficulties do you experience?
- Describe a specific experience working in a group or team situation where there was interpersonal conflict. Describe how you approached the conflict, what worked well, and what did not. How did you manage the outcome?

▶ Communication Skills

o Tell me about a situation in which you had to speak up or be assertive in order to get an important point across.

o How would you define good communication skills?

o How would you rate your communication skills? What have you done to improve them?

o Describe a time when you had to change your communication style to deliver a message or get your point across.

o Describe the most important document, report, or presentation that you had to complete.

o Give me some examples of how you have adapted your own style to deal with different people and situations.

o Would you rather write a report or give a verbal report? Why?

o How would you rate your writing abilities? Your listening skills?

o Describe a time when you tried to persuade another person to do something that he/she was not eager to do.

o Describe a situation in which you experienced ineffective communication. What would you do differently in this situation?

o Sell me this pen (bottle of water, computer, etc.).

▶ Management Skills

o Give an example of what you've done when your time schedule or project plan was upset by unforeseen circumstances.

o Tell me about a recent crisis you handled.

o Do you work well under pressure? Can you make fast decisions?

o Do you manage your time well?

o How do you handle different priorities in your life (e.g., family, work, school, sports)?

o Describe a situation in which you recognized a problem or an opportunity. How did you respond? Did you choose to address this situation on your own? What obstacles did you face and how did you overcome them?

o How do you make important decisions?

o How do you manage risk?

o What do you do when you are having trouble with a project?

o What was your most difficult decision in the last six months? What made it difficult?

o Your boss (client) tells you to do something you believe is wrong. What do you do?

o Describe a situation in which you had to make an important decision without having all the necessary information at hand.

o Describe a situation demonstrating your ability to transition quickly and effectively between different tasks.

o How did you shift priorities and modify actions to meet changing job demands on short notice?

o How did you prepare for this interview?

▸ **Capacity to Learn**

o Describe a difficult situation that you feel you should have handled differently. What did you learn from that experience?

o You have had little experience with marketing (finance, technology, etc.). How do you intend to learn what is required from the position you are applying for?

o How do you handle change?

o Are your grades a good measure of your ability to learn?

o If hired, you will be working with experienced individuals who have been with the company for many years. What makes you think that your performance will be on a par with theirs?

o In what areas do you need to develop professionally? How do you plan to achieve that?

▸ **Drive**

o Give me examples of projects or tasks you started on your own.

o Give me an example of how you demonstrated initiative.

o What are your most important long-term goals? What aspirations do you have for yourself over the next five or so years — professionally and personally?

o Where do you see yourself in two (five, ten) years?

o What does "success" ("failure") mean to you?

o Describe a situation in which you aspired to reach a goal. What obstacles confronted you along the way? What did you do to overcome them?

o Tell me about a time you hit a wall trying to push forward a great idea.

o Describe a situation that demanded sustained, unusually hard work, where others might have thought you couldn't succeed. Was the experience stressful? If so, how did you handle the stress?

Questions Testing Your Functional Knowledge

There are two basic types of functional knowledge questions: questions probing your theoretical knowledge (e.g., frameworks, models, and concepts) and questions calling for specific examples to illustrate a particular concept. Examples of common interview questions from each of these two types are given below.

▸ **Conceptual Questions**

○ You're launching a new product line for our company. Walk me through your decision on how to structure pricing (advertising, distribution, service).

○ A brand is very powerful in one product category of the supermarket. How do you determine whether to leverage the brand in another category? (i.e., Should Coke enter the ice cream market?)

○ How do you determine whether or not to extend your product line?

○ If your brand manager asks you to write a marketing plan for the next year, what would the table of contents look like?

○ Which is more profitable, a 10% increase in price or a 10% increase in share?

○ What would you do to double a company's market share?

○ What are the 10 most important questions that you would ask to learn about a brand on your first day of work as a brand manager?

○ You are the brand manager of Company X and you need a new product to drive the top line. Where do you go?

○ How would you evaluate the success of an advertising campaign?

○ Is Super Bowl advertising a good value?

▸ **Example Questions**

○ Name a product you think is marketed (advertised) well.

○ Identify one good and one bad commercial.

○ Identify a website that markets consumer goods well.

○ Identify a brand that you feel is (is not) marketed well. Why is it (isn't it) marketed well?

○ Tell me about a new product introduction you liked. What would you have done differently to market the product?

○ Tell me about a poor product that was marketed well. What would you have done differently to the product?

○ Identify a company that has made a huge strategic error. Why was it an error?

Questions Testing Your Fit with the Company

There are three basic dimensions of your fit with the company: personality fit, commitment to the company, and commitment to the functional area. Examples of common interview questions from each of these types are given below.

▸ **Personality Fit**

o What experiences/skills do you feel are particularly transferable to our organization?

o What type of work do you like to do best?

o What accomplishments have given you the greatest satisfaction?

o Describe one of your most defining experiences.

o What was the most important thing your parents (prior job experiences) taught you?

o Other than money, what makes you happy at work?

o If you could have dinner with anyone, dead or alive, who would it be and why?

o How do you spend your spare time? What is your favorite hobby? Name a book you've recently read. What movies have you recently seen?

o Have you heard anything about our company that you do not like?

o How would you fit with our corporate culture?

o What do you consider more important: a high salary or career advancement?

o What characteristics should we be looking for in the "ideal" candidate for our company?

▸ **Commitment to the Company**

o Why would you choose our firm over our competitors?

o Why do you want to work for our company?

o How long do you plan to stay with our company?

o Is there anything that will prevent you from taking a position with our company?

o With what other firms are you interviewing?

o Which other industries are you considering?

o Which of our company's products would you like to market? Why?

o Who is our main competitor?

o How would you improve the performance of our company?

o Where do you think our industry is going? What are the key trends and how would they impact our company?

▸ **Interest in the Functional Area**

o Why would you like to pursue a career in consulting (marketing)?

o Why are you interested in marketing/brand management?

o What brands do you feel passionately about and why?

o Which three items would you take with you to "Brand Manager Island"?

Discussing Strengths, Weaknesses, and Mistakes

Some of the most common interview questions involve asking candidates to identify their strengths, weaknesses, successes, and mistakes. Examples of such questions and possible answer strategies are given below.

○ Identify your key *strengths*.

This is an easy question for most candidates. The key issue here is to underscore the strengths that fit the company needs.

There are many variations of the same question: What makes you special? How would you describe yourself? How would your friends (teammates, boss) describe you? If you had a blank billboard on which to create an ad for yourself, how would you fill the billboard? If you created an advertisement for yourself for this position, what would it be like? Which brand best fits your personality and why? Describe your strengths and how you would position yourself in the marketplace.

○ Identify your key *weaknesses*.

This is a difficult, as well as a very tricky, question. Everyone has weaknesses, but you do not want them to hinder your chance of getting an offer. There is no common approach to this question; however, it is important to have a ready answer.

As a general rule, you might consider not emphasizing weaknesses that reflect a major deficiency in the skills required for the position you are applying for, weaknesses that could potentially result in significant damage to your employer, and weaknesses for which you cannot clearly articulate how you intend to successfully overcome their potential limitations.

One possible answer strategy when talking about your weaknesses is to state that you have no shortcomings that will prevent you from doing an excellent job and being an asset to your interviewer's company. An alternative strategy is to put a positive spin on the question: Instead of talking about weaknesses, identify areas in which you are likely to perform your best (which implicitly identifies some areas in which you might not be that strong). In most cases, it is a good idea to avoid clichés of the type: "I work too much."

Overall, it is important to keep in mind that selectively identifying your weaknesses has important ethical implications. Thus, if you think that you have major deficiencies, instead of hiding them from your employer, you should consider working on them to improve your performance prior to the interview.

○ What are your three (two, one) most important *accomplishments*? Why?

This is a straightforward question: Pick accomplishments that most clearly communicate your value to the company.

○ What is your greatest *failure*?

This is another difficult question requiring a well-thought-out answer. The goal is to identify a failure that does not hinder your chance of getting an offer. In general, you might want to avoid failures that resulted in a significant damage (e.g., financial loss, negative publicity, loss of a client) to your employer, failures that reflect a major deficiency in the skills required for the position you are applying for, failures that are too recent and from which you have not had a chance to learn, as well as failures for which you cannot clearly articulate the lessons learned and, instead, provide an example of a scenario in which you successfully resolved a similar problem.

One strategy to address this question is to embed your failure in a context that turns this failure into a valuable experience. This approach, summarized in Figure 7, calls for a brief description of the failure, which is then followed by a summary of the lessons learned from that experience and a success story demonstrating how you applied the lessons learned from the failure to your advantage. Conclude your story by identifying how the lessons learned from your failure enhances your value to the company.

Figure 7: Framing a Failure as a Learning Experience

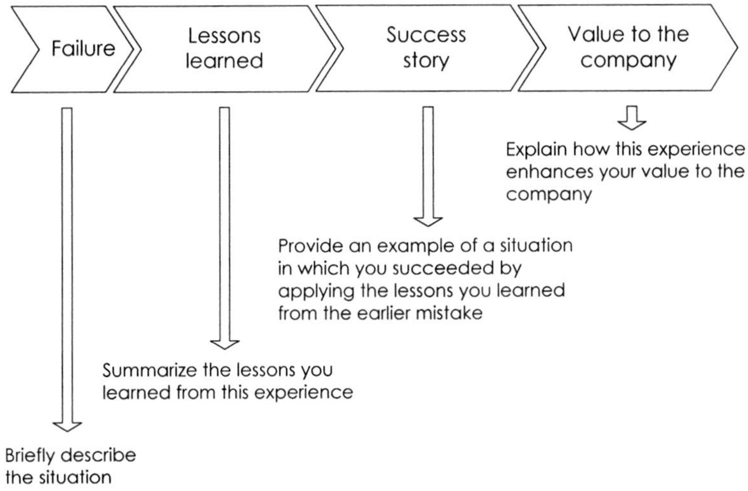

Failure ⟩ Lessons learned ⟩ Success story ⟩ Value to the company

Explain how this experience enhances your value to the company

Provide an example of a situation in which you succeeded by applying the lessons you learned from the earlier mistake

Summarize the lessons you learned from this experience

Briefly describe the situation

Chapter Four

The Case Interview

Being a successful manager requires the ability to deal creatively with complex problems and to reach logical conclusions based on the available facts in a short timeframe. Because no particular background or set of qualifications prepares candidates for that, many companies have come to rely on the case analysis approach as an integral part of the interview process.

Case interviews test your ability to solve problems on the spot. Case analysis not only allows interviewers to examine your ability to think logically and articulate an answer, it also allows them to observe your thought processes, tolerance for ambiguity and data overload, poise, self-confidence, and communication skills under pressure. For that reason, case analysis is an important part of the interview. As an additional benefit, the interactive nature of the case interview adds a dynamic dimension to understanding your personality and allows better evaluation of your fit with the interviewer's company.

Case analysis can involve two types of problems: business cases and brainteasers. Business cases deal with business problems such as profitability, market share, mergers and acquisitions, new product launch decisions, etc. Brainteasers, in contrast, deal with logical problems across different, typically non-business, contexts. These two types of cases are discussed in more detail in the following sections.

Business Cases

Case analysis examines your approach to a complex situation and tests skills and competencies to identify and solve complex problems. Case analysis places particular emphasis on factors that are more difficult to test in the context of the traditional interview. These factors include logical reasoning and quantitative analysis (analytical skills), creative problem solving (creativity), the ability to clearly express your point of view (communication skills), and professional poise and ability to perform under pressure (management skills).

In a case interview, you are introduced to a particular business scenario and asked to analyze the situation and offer a solution. The interview proceeds as an open dialogue between you and the interviewer in which your goal is to identify the source of the problem and recommend a solution.

The key issue to keep in mind is that case analysis is not about the solution per se; it is about how you arrive at that solution. Rather than looking for one specific answer, interviewers are trying to understand how you think. In this context, the interviewer is more interested in your assumptions, your selection of a framework, and the quality of your reasoning than in whether you arrive at the "right answer" (which, as a matter of fact, often does not exist).

A good strategy for approaching case analysis is to think of the interview as a problem-solving task in which you work through hypothetical business problems. Try to forget that this is an interview and think of it as a consulting assignment in which the interviewer is the client. Your goal should be to solve your client's problem rather than guess at the "right" answer. Remember that the interviewer wants to hire a person who will be solving business problems on a day-to-day basis and feels comfortable with the process.

Business Case Format

Business cases can be presented in one of two formats: oral and written. These two formats are discussed in more detail below.

Oral cases are presented in an interactive manner: They offer very little information up front and leave it up to you to uncover the case specifics. Oral cases are very popular among recruiters, especially during the early rounds of interviews, because they provide excellent insights into candidates' ability to identify the relevant information, decision processes, and interpersonal skills. Business problems are often phrased as "CEO questions" or "client questions." For example: "You are the CEO of a telecommunications company and your profits are falling despite the overall category growth. What do you do?" or "You have been hired to advise a major consumer goods company that is considering launching a new line of lunch cereals. How would you advise your client?"

In addition to the typical business problems, interviews can involve behavioral cases that deal with relationship-building and team-management issues. A common behavioral case involves a client project in which something has gone wrong, and the goal is to resolve the problem, control the damage, and deal with the team and/or the client. You might be asked to explain what you will do to resolve the situation or, alternatively, you might be asked to role play the interaction.

Written cases are usually several pages long and are accompanied by data exhibits that contain supplemental information. Candidates are usually given time to read the case and prepare for a discussion. Written cases offer insights into your ability for logical reasoning and quantitative skills, as well as the ability to interpret complex data patterns, usually presented in the form of a chart and/or a table. The goal is to assess candidates' ability to interpret data presented in different formats and their ability to derive conclusions from these data. This type of case is often used by recruiters during advanced rounds of the interview, although some consulting companies tend to use written cases during the early rounds as well.

Written cases can also be tested in both an individual and group context. In a group case analysis, each of the candidates is given a written case and a set of specific questions to be answered. After reading the case, candidates take part in a group discussion in which they present their solution and comment on the solutions presented by other team members. Recruiters are looking for candidates who can present their own findings, integrate the input from other team members, and comment on the solutions presented by other team members. In this context, group interviews are a litmus test for your leadership abilities, interpersonal skills, and collaborative spirit.

How to Approach the Case

The case interview typically starts with a brief description of a business scenario such as a client facing declining market share, eroding profit margins, or a new product introduction. Recruiters are not looking for candidates who happen to know the right answer and can "crack the case," but rather for people who have a system that will allow them to solve *any* case. Indeed, even though each problem requires its own unique analysis, most companies believe that the process of analyzing various business problems has a common structure that carries across different scenarios. Therefore, when discussing the case, it is important to apply a logical, well-structured approach that enables you to reach a meaningful conclusion.

A common approach to case analysis includes four steps: clarify, structure, analyze, and conclude. These four steps to case analysis are logically connected (Figure 1). First, determine the situation, identify the problem, and verify the facts; next, develop and present a framework for analyzing the problem; then, apply the framework to analyze specific problems and derive effective solutions; and finally, make a recommendation. These steps are outlined in more detail below.

Figure 1. Structuring the Case Analysis

o *Clarify.* The first step is to make sure that you understand the business scenario and the question you are being asked. In fact, one of the most common mistakes during a case interview is misunderstanding the question or answering the wrong question. Sometimes the interviewer will deliberately interject ambiguity into the problem as a part of the interview. Ask clarification questions if you are unclear about certain aspects of the case. A simple strategy to start case analysis is to paraphrase the question to ensure that you understand the problem.

o *Structure.* Structuring involves choosing an approach (framework) to solve the problem. It is a good idea to describe your overall approach and explain the logic used to address the problem. Try to find the appropriate framework to break the problem into separate issues, but do not force-fit a framework to the problem. Remember that your goal is not to showcase your knowledge of a particular framework but to demonstrate your ability to solve business problems. Frameworks are tools to help you organize your thinking; they are not the solution to the problem. It is a good idea to explain the reasons for selecting the framework you use and how you would go about applying the framework to the problem at hand. Remember that recruiters are not particularly interested in your solution to the problem at hand; instead, they are interested in your ability to apply a systematic approach to solving diverse business problems. Because of its complexity, the issue of using frameworks in case analysis is addressed in more detail in the second part of this book.

o *Analyze.* There are three basic components to a solid analysis: facts, assumptions, and logic.

- *Facts* are the cornerstones of your analysis and are used to derive your assumptions, logical conclusions, and proposed actions. Some of the facts might not be readily available, and you will have to ask the interviewer to fill in the gaps. As a general rule, the shorter the case, the greater the likelihood that you will have to request additional information as you analyze the problem.

- *Assumptions* are necessary to fill in the missing facts. Making assumptions is a common practice in business analysis; the key is to ensure that your assumptions are realistic and clearly articulated. Use sensitivity analysis (e.g., compare an aggressive vs. a conservative scenario) when unsure about the validity of a particular assumption (e.g., market share growth, rate of new product adoption).

- *Logic* links the available information (facts and assumptions) to uncover new relationships (e.g., cause-and-effect), derive conclusions (e.g., if … then…), and/or apply general business principles to the case at hand (e.g., an increase in price is likely to lead to a decrease in quantity sold). Break the problem into separate issues, address the issues one at a time, and state findings for each analysis. Remember that the interview is not about the outcome (i.e., getting the "right" answer) but about the process of getting the problem solved. Walk the interviewer through your thinking, and use visual aids (flowchart, matrix, bullet points) when possible.

o *Conclude.* Conclude the case discussion by summarizing your logic and offering a recommendation that reflects your decision on how the company should address the situation described in the case. The proposed solution should be clear and based on your evaluation of facts, assumptions, and logic, rather than on unsubstantiated opinions. Link your recommendation back to the problem and identify how your solution will solve the problem.

Brainteaser Cases

Brainteaser questions seek to directly test your creative problem-solving and logical reasoning skills. While not all interviewers use brainteasers, they are very common among management consulting and software companies. Unlike traditional business cases, brainteasers usually are abstract questions describing a specific, typically non-business problem. Although some questions might require certain factual knowledge, most brainteasers are self-contained logical tasks. There are three main types of brainteasers: (1) estimation cases (e.g., How many piano tuners are there in the world?), (2) logical cases (e.g., Why do Coke cans have an indent on the bottom?), and (3) creative cases (e.g., How would you move Mount Fuji?). These three types of brainteasers are described in more detail in the following sections.

Estimation Cases

The popularity of estimation cases in management consulting interviews stems from the fact that these questions are not only easy to create, discuss, and evaluate, but also that they are representative of the type of problems managers and consultants face in their day-to-day work. Estimation questions typically require both logical deduction and quantitative skills. Their goal is not to test factual knowledge but, instead, to observe your approach to problem solving. In this context, the answer, per se, is often irrelevant; what counts is the process of arriving at the answer.

Estimation cases can vary from market sizing problems in which you have to determine the size of a particular market (e.g., What is the size of the market for the Segway human transporter?) to estimating physical factors such as weight and volume (e.g., How much does the moon weigh?).

Estimation tasks can sometimes be part of a more comprehensive case analysis. To illustrate, the answer to the question of whether a company should launch a new product largely depends on the size of the potential market.

While each estimation question is likely to have its unique set of solutions, two general approaches to estimation questions can be identified: analysis and analogy.

o *Estimation by analysis* involves breaking down the object into smaller parts and estimating each part individually. For example, in the case of estimating the weight of an airplane, one might break down the problem into a series of more specific tasks such as estimating the weight of the different parts of the airplane: the body, engines, fuel, luggage, passengers, etc.

o *Estimation by analogy* involves comparing the estimated object to a similar object with known parameters. To illustrate, when asked to estimate the number of car batteries annually sold in the United States, one can use total car sales to arrive at the answer.

Estimation cases might require certain factual knowledge to derive the final answer. Knowing the facts helps, but it is not crucial. Remember, the goal of the interview is not to test whether you can get the "right" answer but to test your ability for logical reasoning. Therefore, if you do not have the necessary data readily available, describe the *process* you would use to solve the problem. In most cases, describing the algorithm is more important than running the actual calculations.

Logic Cases

Logic cases typically describe an abstract problem based on logical reasoning. The goal is to uncover the logical principle underlying the problem. Unlike estimation and creative questions, most logical problems have a unique solution. To illustrate, consider the classic problem: Why do Coke cans have an indent on the bottom? More examples of logic questions and solutions can be found at the end of this chapter.

Creative Cases

Creative cases are another form of brainteasers and are very popular among companies in which creativity is paramount (e.g., software, design, product development, and advertising). By definition, creative cases can be about virtually anything. To illustrate, consider the following questions: How would you describe green to a blind person? How would you design a mobile phone for dogs? How would you design a restroom for a CEO? How would you develop a technology to grow straight bananas? How would you describe a pineapple to a person who has never seen one? How would you describe the business school of the future? These questions test your creativity and ability to think "outside of the box" to find an original solution to a non-trivial problem. An additional benefit of creative questions is that they lend themselves to interesting conversation that can provide further insights into your personality.

Preparing for a Brainteaser Interview

Because brainteaser questions lack a pre-set format, topic, and structure, one cannot really "prepare" for a brainteaser interview (which is one of the reasons that interviewers like these questions!). Practicing, however, can help you better articulate your decision process, improve your logical thinking, and help you develop your own strategy for approaching brainteaser questions.

Winning Case Interview Strategies

Mastering the case analysis requires the ability to deal creatively with complex problems and to reach logical conclusions, based on the available information, in a short period of time. The interactive nature of case analysis adds a dynamic dimension to the interview by letting the recruiter observe your poise, self-confidence, and communication skills under pressure. A set of winning strategies on how to manage the problem-solving and the interactive aspects of the case interview are outlined below.

▸ Solving the Case

o Make sure you are answering the question you have been asked; ask questions if you are unsure about the details. Misunderstanding the question or answering the wrong question is one of the most common mistakes in a case interview.

o Remember that rarely are you given all the case information up front. You are expected to ask intelligent questions that will reveal the relevant information that is not readily available.

o Be systematic. Finish one key question and summarize the findings before you go on to the next. Step back periodically to summarize what you have learned so far and how it relates to the problem you are trying to solve. Do not proceed in a haphazard fashion, jumping from one issue to another.

o Use frameworks creatively. Do not force-fit a familiar framework to a problem (one of the most common case analysis mistakes). The key is to use common sense.

o Always focus on the big picture: Solve the problem without getting stuck in details. Prioritize issues. Start with factors that are likely to have the greatest impact. There is no need to mention the framework you will be using by name; instead, explain the structure of your analysis so that the interviewer understands your thought process.

o When given a complex problem, think broadly and be sure to cover all relevant issues rather than spending all your time on one particular issue (unless the interviewer asks you to do so).

o Stay away from phrases like "as we learned in our strategy class..." and "the textbook says that..." to justify your decisions. You should be able to explain and justify the logic for your arguments on your own.

o Do not be afraid to think "outside the box." There is no box. Creativity and brainstorming may be just what the interviewer is seeking. Use business judgment, logic, and common sense.

o Identify the assumptions you are making to solve the problem. Explain the rationale for making these assumptions and their consistency with the facts of the case. Always clarify whether you are making assumptions of your own or restating the case facts.

- When possible, use visual aids to support your analysis. Draw flowcharts to represent business processes; use bullet points to highlight different aspects of the case; use matrixes to represent more complex relationships between factors with multiple levels.

- When possible, use calculations to support your analysis. This is an opportunity to demonstrate your quantitative skills.

▸ Interacting with the Interviewer

- Listen carefully and take notes. Remember that you are not expected to have a ready solution to the case problem; when necessary, take a moment to collect your thoughts.

- Think out loud. The interviewer wants to know your thought process, not just the solution. If you have rejected some alternatives, explain why so that the interviewer has a better understanding of your thought process.

- Structure your answer by explaining your strategy (framework) up front so that the interviewer knows what you are trying to do.

- Be confident, even if you do not know the answer to a specific question. It is important for the interviewer to understand that you know how to react if a client asks you something you do not know.

- Remember that "cracking the case" does not mean finding the "right" answer (which rarely exists). It is all about how you analyze the problem.

- Interact with the interviewer. The case should be a dialogue, not a monologue.

- Be flexible in defending your point. The interviewer might disagree with you in order to test your reaction to being challenged. Keep an open mind and watch for cues from the interviewer.

- Think of the interviewer as your client. The interview is a test of your ability to interact with the client in a way that allows you to better understand the problem, identify its underlying cause, and make a sound recommendation.

- Have fun. Interviewers are looking for people who enjoy solving problems and are fun to work with. Think of case analysis as an opportunity to discuss novel ideas and address challenging problems with smart people.

- The best way to ensure that all of the above issues come to you naturally during the interview is to practice. Practice solving different cases to become more comfortable with the process.

Estimation Cases: Problems and Solutions

Estimation cases are a form of brainteaser commonly given in interviews to test logical thinking and analytical skills.

o How many golf balls does it take to fill up an Olympic swimming pool?

The popular solution is to compare the volume of the swimming pool and the golf ball. Given that the pool is 50 meters x 25 meters x 3 meters, its volume is 3,750 cubic meters, or 228,837,667 cubic inches. The golf ball's volume is 2.48 cubic inches (the radius of the golf ball is 0.84 inches and the formula for measuring the volume of a sphere is: [4 x (Pi) x radius cubed]. Given that the densest packing of spheres possible is 74%, it can be calculated that it takes 68.28 million golf balls to fill the pool. Note, however, that this solution requires very specific knowledge (e.g., the formula for measuring the volume of a sphere and the maximum density packing coefficient) and, hence, is not readily applicable to most business interviews.

An alternative solution does not require knowing complex formulas. The size of an Olympic pool is 50 meters x 25 meters x 3 meters. The diameter of a golf ball is 1.68 inches or .0427 meters (1 inch = 2.54 centimeters). Therefore, it will take 685,000 golf balls to cover the bottom of the pool (1,171 x 585). The depth of the pool is 3 meters or 70 golf balls. Therefore, when golf balls are stacked up by putting each layer precisely on top of one another, the swimming pool will accommodate approximately 47.95 million balls (685,000 x 70). Note, however that a greater efficiency can be achieved by shifting every other layer by 2.1 centimeters (half a golf ball). Assume that it will result in approximately 40% stacking efficiency (which can be illustrated by a simple drawing) – that is, instead of 70 layers of golf balls the pool will accommodate 98 layers (70 x 1.4). Therefore, the total amount of balls the swimming pool can accommodate is about 67.13 million (685,000 x 98).

o How many barbers are there in Chicago?

Chicago's population is close to 3 million → assume 50% are men → assume 6 haircuts per year → 9 million haircuts per year. Assume also that each haircut takes 30 minutes and the average barber works 8 hours a day, 5 days a week, 50 weeks a year (2 weeks vacation) → 4,000 haircuts per year. Therefore, there should be 2,250 barbers (assuming that all men get a haircut from a barber; if this is not the case, then the derived number is overestimated).

▸ Additional Estimation Questions:

o What is the weight of a Boeing 747?

o How many computers are sold daily?

o How many gas stations (pay phones, restaurants) are there in Chicago?

o How would you go about estimating your competitor's budget for advertising/promotional/R&D expenses?

o How many car batteries are sold in the United States each year?

o How many tennis balls can I fit in a football stadium?

- How many rotations does a tire on the front of a family sedan make on a road trip from New York to Boston?
- How many golf balls can fit in the typical suitcase?
- What is the maximum number of pencils I can fit across my desk without stacking them?
- Estimate the speed at which your fingernails grow in miles per hour.
- How much beer is consumed in Germany every year?
- What was the total volume added to landfills in the U.S. because of disposable diapers last year?
- How much tea is there in China?
- At any moment, how many pennies are inside a shopping mall?
- How many two-liter bottles of soda will be sold in the U.S. next year?
- Estimate the number of blades of grass in the average suburban lawn.
- How many hotel-sized bottles of shampoo are produced each year around the world?
- Estimate the number of people born in the world yesterday.
- How many times does the average Forbes 500 CEO hit the key "E" on a keyboard during a day?
- Estimate the number of hairs on your head.
- How tall is this building?
- How long does it take for a light bulb to turn on?
- How much milk is produced in the U.S. each year?
- How many tomatoes does Heinz use in its production of ketchup in one year?
- During the course of a day, how many people walk into London's Heathrow airport?

Logic Cases: Problems and Solutions

Logic cases are a form of brainteaser cases commonly given in interviews to test your ability to deal with abstract problems and to observe your problem-solving process.

o Why are manhole covers round?

A round cover cannot fall into a manhole, whereas square or rectangular ones can (e.g., if placed diagonally). Round manhole covers are also easier to be rolled down the street if necessary.

o Why do Coke cans have an indent at the bottom?

To control can expansion so that, in case of pressure, it does not bulge in the opposite direction or at the sides, which would not allow the can to stand up normally and would make it less visually appealing.

o You are in a room with three light switches. Each one controls one light bulb in the next room. Your goal is to figure out which switch controls which light bulb. You may flick only two switches and may enter into the light bulb room only once.

The key is to realize that a light bulb can also be tested by touch. Flick the first switch, wait for a few minutes, then turn it off and flick the second switch. Enter the light bulb room. The bulb that is on connects to the second switch. The warm light bulb is controlled by the first switch.

o Consider a set of cards, each one having a letter on one side and a number on the other side. You are given a subset of four cards as follows (the upper side): D-K-3-7. You have to test the following rule: If a card has a D on one side, it has a 3 on the other side. You must decide which cards need to be turned over to know whether this sample of cards is consistent with the rule.

The correct cards are D and 7 (although 90% of people pick D and 3). Seeing what is on the reverse of the 7 card can lead to disconfirming the rule if a D shows up (whereas seeing what is on the reverse of the 3 card cannot disconfirm the rule and is, hence, non-informative).[1]

o A bat and a ball cost $1.10 in total. The bat costs $1 more than the ball. How much does the ball cost?

The ball costs five cents (although most people think it is ten cents).[2]

▸ Additional Logic Questions:

o What is the angle between the minute hand and the hour hand at 12:45?

o You have a bucket of three different colored buttons. You are blindfolded and asked to pick up two buttons of the same color. What is the minimum number of buttons you must pick up before you can be sure that you have least two different colored buttons in your hand?

o A special kind of plant doubles in height every year for fifteen years. In what year was it half its maximum height?

- You want to boil an egg for four minutes, but you only have a two-minute and a six-minute hourglass timer. How can you use these two hourglass timers to boil the egg?

- You are a merchant trying to cross a river. In your possession are a coyote, a rabbit, and bucket of freshly picked tomatoes. You have a boat, but you can only take one item at a time to cross the river. The trouble is, the coyote wants to eat the rabbit, and the rabbit wants to eat the tomatoes. How can you get yourself and your merchandise across the river?

- Three men challenge each other to a "truel" (a three sided duel). The three men have varying levels of skill, and the worst gunman is asked to fire first, followed by the intermediate gunman, and finally the best gunman, after which they will continue in this order until there is only one man left standing. Where should the first shooter aim?

- If you are on a boat and you throw a wooden barrel overboard, does the level of water rise, sink, or stay the same?

- A spider is trapped in a slippery bucket. Every day he climbs 15 inches up but slips down 10 inches. The bucket is 25 inches tall. How long does it take for the spider to get out?

- How can you divide a round birthday cake into 8 equal pieces with only 3 straight slices of a knife?

- What is unique about the number 854917632?

- If you put a coin into a bottle and then insert a cork into the bottle's opening, how can you take the coin out without removing the cork or breaking the bottle?

Source

[1] Wason, P. C. (1960), "On the Failure to Eliminate Hypotheses in a Conceptual Task," *Quarterly Journal of Experimental Psychology*, 12, 129-140.

[2] Kahneman, Daniel (2003), "Maps of Bounded Rationality: Psychology for Behavioral Economics Dagger," *American Economic Review*, 93, 1449.

Core Skills Sought by Employers

Most employers look for the same set of attributes in job candidates: core skills (leadership, analytical skills, creativity, teamwork, communication skills, management skills, capacity to learn, and drive), knowledge (functional, industry, and global knowledge), and the overall fit with the company (personality fit, commitment to the company, and interest in the functional area). Even though they look for the same skill set, companies vary in the way they articulate these skills. Following is a sample of the key skills sought by companies in the three most popular recruiting areas: consulting, marketing, and finance.[1]

▸ **Concentration in Consulting**

AT Kearney

o Perceptive

o Resourceful

o Achieving

o Teaming

Bain & Company

o Intelligence

o Integrity

o Passion

o Ambition

Booz Allen Hamilton

o Critical thinking and problem solving

o Creativity

o Quantitative analytics

o Conceptual analytics

o Business and personal leadership

o Interpersonal skills

o Intellect, knowledge, and insight

o Interest

DiamondCluster International

o Strong analytical and problem solving skills

o Ability to add value and influence change

o Ability to work effectively in a team environment

o Demonstrated initiative and leadership

o Strong written and verbal communication skills

o Creativity and resourcefulness

o Honesty and integrity

o Commitment and reliability

o Adaptability and flexibility

Grant Thornton

o Hard working

o Creative

o Passion for excellence

o Integrity

o Teamwork

Kurt Salmon Associates

o Integrity

o Drive to excel

o Strong analytical and communication skills

o Personal resilience

o Team players

o Commitment

L.E.K. Consulting

o Intelligence

o Honesty

o Hard work

o Integrity

o Teamwork

- Good humor

Marakon Associates

- Structured and logical thinking
- A creative and analytical approach to problem solving
- Empathy, maturity, and professionalism
- An understanding of the business issues confronting CEOs and general management
- Ability to work and communicate effectively with clients and colleagues at all levels
- Desire to achieve high standards both personally and professionally
- Common sense

Mars & Company

- Strong quantitative skills
- Energy
- Maturity
- Creativity
- Uncommon common sense
- A sense of humor

McKinsey & Company

- Problem solving
- Achieving
- Personal impact
- Leadership

Mercer Management Consulting

- The ability to structure problems logically
- The ability to develop innovative yet practical solutions
- The ability to work effectively as members of a team
- The ability to communicate clearly with both colleagues and clients
- The ability to take initiative and leadership both internally and with clients

Monitor Group

- Capabilities
- Capacity to learn

○ Commitment

ZS Associates

○ Analytical and quantitative skills

○ Strategic thinking

○ Personal presence

○ Business acumen

○ Strong communication skills

○ Commitment

○ Collegiality

○ Creativity

▸ **Concentration in Marketing**

American Express

○ Ability to develop winning strategies and drive results

○ Strong focus on customer and client service

○ Personal excellence

○ Ability to drive innovation and change

○ Ability to build important relationships

○ Ability to communicate effectively across diverse global teams

Clorox

○ Talent

○ Drive

○ Focus on results

○ Innovation

○ Team player

○ Leadership

○ Passion

Gillette

○ Organizational excellence

○ Achievement

○ Integrity

- Collaboration

Microsoft

- Long-term approach
- Strategic thinking
- Passion for products and technology
- Customer focus
- Individual excellence
- Team spirit
- Interpersonal skills

PepsiCo

- Results orientation
- Commitment to excellence
- Willingness to learn
- Sense of excitement
- Ability to innovate
- Intelligence
- Dedication

Procter & Gamble

- Leadership
- Risk-taking
- Innovation
- Solutions
- Collaboration
- Mastery

SC Johnson

- Leadership
- High initiative
- Analytical ability
- Teamwork skills
- Creativity

- ○ Innovation

Unilever

- ○ Determination to win
- ○ Business focus
- ○ Intellectual skills
- ○ People skills
- ○ Integrity

▸ **Concentration in Finance**

CitiGroup

- ○ Integrity
- ○ Excellence
- ○ Respect
- ○ Teamwork
- ○ Ownership
- ○ Leadership

Deutsche Bank

- ○ Customer focus
- ○ Teamwork
- ○ Innovation
- ○ Performance
- ○ Trust
- ○ Passion to perform

Fidelity Investments

- ○ Understanding of the financial services industry
- ○ Knowledge of accounting and financial principles
- ○ Ability to work effectively with senior executives
- ○ Strong analytical skills
- ○ Excellent time management skills
- ○ Ability to organize, prioritize, and multi-task
- ○ Excellent project management and presentation skills

Goldman Sachs

- Passion for excellence
- Belief in the power of the group
- Integrity
- Trust
- Leadership
- Desire to be challenged
- Drive

Lehman Brothers

- Problem solving and analytic ability
- Leadership
- Initiative
- Team player
- Self confidence
- Assertiveness
- Maturity
- Ability to interact with others, persuade, and listen
- Recognition of own strengths and weaknesses

Morgan Stanley

- Energetic
- Creative
- Well-rounded
- Outgoing
- Self-motivated
- Ability to learn quickly
- Strong quantitative and analytical skills
- Desire to thrive in a dynamic, high-pressure environment

UBS Investment Bank

- Problem analysis
- Judgment and decision making
- Innovation

- Communication and impact
- Drive and commitment
- Teamwork
- Planning and organizing

Note

[1] For up-to-date information about the recruitment processes, please obtain the necessary information directly from the company.

Part Two

Mastering the Case Analysis

The Case Interview

A popular strategy used to prepare for case interviews is to read numerous transcripts of real interviews. While familiarizing yourself with a few specific examples of case interviews is definitely helpful, one of the biggest problems with relying exclusively on transcripts is that it is virtually impossible to prepare in advance for all the possible questions you might be asked during the interview. Companies are not looking for applicants who have memorized a set of specific case solutions but rather for individuals who understand the logic underlying the solution and who can apply this logic to solving new problems. Therefore, instead of simply offering transcripts from past interviews, this book introduces a systematic approach to business problem-solving, complemented with focused case discussions.

Based on the nature of the underlying task, most cases can be divided into three basic types: (1) action-planning cases, (2) performance-gap cases, and (3) external-change cases.

Action-planning cases typically involve the development of a course of action to achieve a certain goal. To illustrate, action-planning cases involve elements such as developing an overall marketing plan for launching a new product offering and developing a pricing, communication, and/or distribution strategy.

Performance-gap cases depict a company faced with a discrepancy between the desired and the actual state of affairs, between the goal and the reality. To illustrate, a decline in an offering's market share can be viewed as a performance gap between the company's desire to strengthen its market position (goal) and the decrease in market share (reality). Other examples of performance gaps include discrepancies between desired and actual net income, profit margins, and revenues.

External-change cases depict a company faced with a change in the environment in which it operates. To illustrate, external change cases involve questions such as evaluating the impact of a new competitive entry, a competitive action (e.g., new product introduction, price change, aggressive promotions, superiority claims), changes in customer demand, changes in technology, legal regulations, and government policies.

These three types of cases can be fairly specific and involve a particular product or service from a given company (e.g., pricing a new product). Alternatively, they can be more general in scope and involve the entire company (e.g., developing a company-wide growth strategy or evaluating the viability of an acquisition). Because individual offerings are the building blocks of a company's overall business strategy, in the following sections we first discuss offering-specific cases (Chapters 5–7) and then discuss cases concerning the entire company (Chapter 8). Finally, we explore a subset of the above cases that offer pre-identified solutions and require explicit evaluation of the viability of the proposed solutions (Chapter 9).

Chapter Five

Solving Action-Planning Cases

Overview

Action-planning cases typically entail the development of a course of action to achieve a certain goal. To illustrate, action-planning cases involve questions about developing an overall marketing plan for launching a new offering and developing a branding, pricing, communication, and/or distribution strategy. Typical examples of action-planning cases are given below.

- *You are charged with marketing a candy bar that has been very successful in France. What things should you consider in bringing the product to market in the United States?*

- *Your client has asked you to help him optimize his product line. How do you approach this assignment?*

- *A start-up software company is preparing to launch its first product. How should it balance customer service and sales force resources?*

- *Your client has developed a new statistical software package. How would you price it?*

- *A music company has asked your advice on how to price a soon-to-be-released record of a new artist. How would you respond?*

- *Your client, AT&T, is trying to determine which customer segments it should target in order to increase revenues. What would you advise?*

- *Your client is considering launching a new product. What should you consider in bringing the product to market?*

- *How would you go about developing a pricing strategy for a large ski resort?*

- *Your client is ready to launch a new product that is both a pen and a USB flash drive. Should she distribute this product to office supply stores or to computer stores?*

- *The CEO of a start-up biotech company has asked your advice in developing a business plan. How would you approach this assignment?*

- *A company has many product upgrades but is finding it hard to encourage customers to buy the new product because the original is still useful. How would you encourage customers to buy new upgrades of the product?*

○ *A department store in Chicago is buying an equally prestigious department store in another city and changing that store's name to match its own. How would you handle changing the name of the store?*

○ *You are the CEO of a Fortune 500 company that is spending $500M on advertising each year. How do you know if this is a worthwhile investment? What would you do next year? Would you increase the advertising budget, decrease it, or leave it unchanged?*

Solving Action-Planning Cases

Most action-planning cases can be solved by applying a relatively simple approach referred to as the G-S-T-I-C framework. The key aspects of this framework are discussed in more detail in the following sections.

The G-S-T-I-C Framework

Central to this framework is the notion that an offering's ultimate success in the market is determined by the soundness of the five key components of its business model, illustrated in Figure 1: goal, strategy, tactics, implementation, and control (G-S-T-I-C).

Figure 1. The G-S-T-I-C Framework for Action Planning

The G-S-T-I-C framework implies that the actions a manager takes on a day-to-day basis (e.g., product and service design, branding, pricing, managing sales promotions and communications, setting up a distribution network) should follow directly from the company's overall strategy, which, in turn, should enable the company to achieve its goal. In this context, developing and/or analyzing an action plan involves the following five steps: (1) set a goal, (2) develop the strategy, (3) design the tactics, (4) develop the implementation plan, and (5) identify the control metrics to measure the proposed action's success. These five steps are outlined in more detail below.

▸ Set a Goal

Every action that a company undertakes should be consistent with a well-defined goal. Setting a goal involves two decisions: identifying the focus of the company's actions and defining the specific performance benchmarks to be achieved. The *focus* identifies the ultimate criterion for a company's success (e.g., net income, profit margins, sales revenues, and market share). *Benchmarks* define the quantitative and temporal aspects of the goal. For example, a goal might involve increasing earnings-per-share (focus) by five percent (quantitative benchmark) by the end of the fiscal year (temporal benchmark).

▸ Develop the Strategy

Strategy outlines the master plan of the company's actions aimed at achieving its goal. Strategy development involves two key components: identifying the market structure and designing the offering's value proposition. The *market structure* depicts the key market participants – target customers, the company, its collaborators and competitors – as well as the overall environment in which the company operates. The five components of market structure are often referred to as the 5-C framework (company, customers, collaborators, competitors, and context). The second aspect of developing the strategy – designing the offering's *value proposition* – aims to maximize the offering's benefits to customers, collaborators, and the company. The processes of identifying market structure and designing a value proposition are discussed in more detail later in this chapter.

▸ Design the Tactics

Tactics identify how the desired strategy is translated into a set of specific actions. Designing the tactics involves identifying three key aspects of the value-management process: *creating, communicating,* and *delivering value* (also referred to as the C-C-D framework). The processes of creating, communicating, and delivering value are implemented through a set of specific marketing activities, commonly referred to as the marketing mix. In general, seven key marketing mix factors can be identified: product, service, brand, price, incentives, communication, and distribution. The role of these factors in designing an offering's tactics is discussed in more detail later in this chapter.

▸ Develop the Implementation Plan

The implementation component of market planning outlines the timeline and the logistics of executing the offering's strategy and tactics. Implementation analysis involves two key decisions: defining the processes that enable the company to implement its strategy and tactics (e.g., product development practices, service delivery infrastructure, brand-building mechanisms, and distribution channel structure) and identifying the people managing these processes (e.g., the core skills and knowledge of the company personnel).

▸ Identify the Control Metrics

To ensure successful implementation of its strategy and tactics, a company must establish controls to monitor its progress toward the goals. Controls involve evaluating the viability of the company's goals, assessing the soundness of the company's strategy and tactics, and monitoring the effectiveness of implementing the business plan. Controls also involve monitoring changes in the environment (e.g., competitive actions) to enable the company to identify potential opportunities and threats and, when necessary, adjust its business activities to better reflect the new market reality.

The two key aspects of the G-S-T-I-C analysis – strategy and tactics – are discussed in more detail in the following sections.

Strategy Analysis

Strategy outlines the master plan of the actions aimed at achieving the company's goal. Strategy development involves two key components: identifying the market structure and defining the offering's value proposition.

Market structure describes the environment in which a given product or service exists. Market structure involves the following five factors: (1) *customers* targeted by a particular offering, (2) the *company* introducing and managing the offering, (3) *collaborators* working with the company on this offering, (4) *competitors* with offerings that provide similar benefits to the target customers, and (5) the social, technological, economic, political, legal, and physical *context* in which the company operates. These five factors, often referred to as the "Five Cs," are summarized in more detail below.

- *Customers.* Identifying target customers involves two decisions: (1) identifying the relevant customer *needs* to be fulfilled by the company's offering and (2) identifying actionable strategies to *reach* customers with these needs (e.g., demographic, geographic, psychographic, and behavioral characteristics that enable the company to communicate and deliver the offering to these customers in an effective and cost-efficient manner).

- *Company.* Company analysis involves identifying available resources and capabilities, such as strategic assets and core competencies. *Strategic assets* are resources that are essential for the success of the business in which the company operates and that differentiate this company from its competitors. *Core competencies* refer to a company's distinct areas of expertise that are critical to achieving a sustainable competitive advantage. Core competencies typically are a result of focused utilization of a company's strategic assets. To illustrate, Dell's core competency in build-to-order delivery stems from its strategic assets such as business infrastructure, collaborator networks, and human capital.

- *Collaborators.* Collaborators are entities that work with the company to create, communicate, or deliver a particular offering. Collaboration might occur in several areas: product, service, brand, price, incentives, communications, and distribution. To illustrate, companies can collaborate to develop a product (research-and-development collaboration); to create a customer incentive (promotional collaboration); and/or to deliver the offering to the customer (channel collaboration).

- *Competitors.* Competitive analysis involves identifying entities with offerings positioned to deliver value to the same customers. Because competitors are defined relative to the needs of the target segment, the competition often goes beyond the traditional industry-defined categories. To illustrate, Coca-Cola competes not only with other cola producers such as Pepsi, but also with producers of all products that could potentially fulfill the same need: juice, bottled water, and milk. In this context, juice, bottled water, and milk are not just substitute products but rather cross-category competitors because they compete to satisfy the same need of the same target customers.

○   *Context.* Context includes factors that describe the relevant aspects of the environment in which the company delivers its offering to customers. Typical context factors include the social, technological, economic, political, legal, and physical environment in which the marketing exchange takes place. The key factors influencing each of these aspects are as follows:

- The *social context* involves demographic factors such as race, age, income, education, and employment.

- The *technological context* involves the technologies that are either directly related to the offering or can result in substitute products.

- The *economic context* involves factors such as the general economic conditions, rate of inflation, interest rates, and rate of unemployment.

- The *political context* involves issues such as political stability of the government, the country and the region; the general business and political orientation of the government; as well as the role of the government in supporting/protecting specific industries.

- The *legal context* involves the legal and regulatory factors that either directly or indirectly affect the offering. To illustrate, the demand for hands-free devices is affected by the legislation in many cities requiring hands-free mobile phone use while driving.

- The *physical context* involves issues such as the overall climate, geographic, and health factors. To illustrate, the demand for a cold medicine is likely to be affected by the flu season, and ice cream consumption is likely to be affected by the weather.

To achieve success, an offering should provide a superior (relative to the competition) *value proposition* to its target customers in a way that enables the company and its collaborators to reach their strategic goals. The three aspects of an offering's value proposition – customer value, collaborator value, and company value – can be better understood when considered in the context of the underlying market structure, as illustrated in Figure 2. Thus, strategy involves defining an offering's value proposition in a way that delivers superior (relative to the competition) value to target customers, the company, and its collaborators in a particular context.

Figure 2. The 5-C Framework for Strategy Analysis

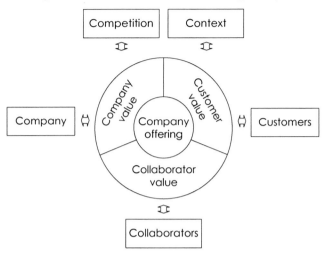

The key aspects of strategic analysis can be illustrated using the example of i-Pod, the digital music player from Apple.

o iPod's primary target *customers* are individuals with the need to have mobile access to music and video recordings. Most of these customers are teenagers and young adults, able to afford iPod's price tag. To these customers, iPod offers a revolutionary digital music player that lets them store music and video content in their pocket and listen/view it wherever they go.

o Apple's *collaborators* include companies like PortalPlayer, which provided the firmware and software platform for the iPod, and Pixo, which was contracted to develop the design and the user interface. These collaborators have benefited from Apple's technological and marketing expertise, as well as from its financial backing. Apple's collaborators also include content providers such as Sony, EMI, Universal, and Warner record labels. For these collaborators, iPod/iTunes offer an alternative distribution channel to reach a desirable target audience. Apple's collaborators also include a diverse set of retailers: mass-merchandisers such as Wal-Mart and Costco, consumer-electronics retailers such as Circuit City and Best Buy, as well as specialized Apple resellers. Among its distributors, iPod creates value by attracting customers to their stores and helping them increase their sales revenues and net income.

o From a *company's* perspective, iPod builds on Apple's core competency of customer-focused product development and Apple's strategic assets, such as technological, design, and marketing expertise, its existing customer base, and the power of its brand. For Apple, iPod delivers value by (1) offering a steady stream of revenues and net income, and (2) providing a platform for product development that enabled Apple to extend its digital-player product line (e.g., iPod Shuffle and iPod Nano) as well as to launch revolutionary new products such as the iPhone.

o iPod *competitors* include Zune (Microsoft), Zen (Creative Labs), Sansa (Sandisk), and Insignia (Best Buy), which offer similar benefits and target the same customers. To be successful, iPod needs to deliver superior value to its target customers and collaborators.

o iPod's success is also a function of the *context* in which it is being sold and used. Among the relevant context factors for iPod are the changes in the overall economy (because it determines consumers' disposable income) the technological developments (e.g., the development of alternative data compression technologies and their compatibility with Apple's proprietary AAC and Apple Lossless formats), as well as regulatory factors (e.g., regulations guiding the copyright and licensing of digital content).

Tactical Analysis

Tactics identify the specific activities employed to execute a given strategy. The tactical aspect of an offering can be represented by the processes of creating, communicating, and delivering value (referred to as the C-C-D framework). The specific activities used to create, communicate, and deliver value are commonly referred to as the marketing mix. In this context, seven key marketing mix factors can be identified: product, service, brand, price, incentives, communication, and distribution. These seven marketing mix factors can be related to the processes of creating, communicating, and delivering value, as shown in Figure 3. Here, the product, service, brand, price, and incentives comprise the value-creation aspect of the offering; communication captures the value-communication aspect; and distribution reflects the value-delivery aspect of the value management process.

Figure 3. Tactical Analysis: The C-C-D Value Management Framework

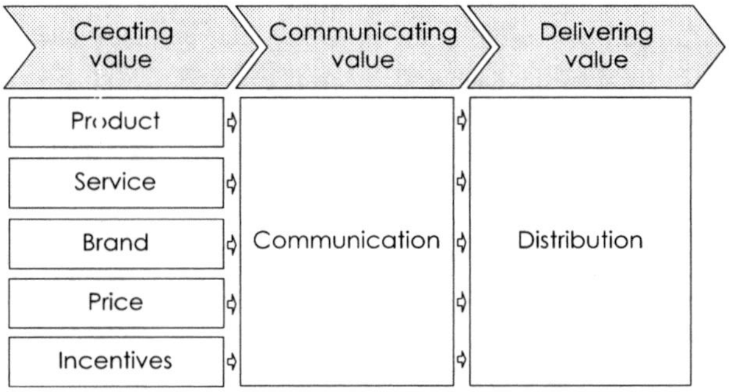

To illustrate, the product aspect of the iPod is the functionality offered by the digital player, such as hard-drive capacity, display, battery life, design, and user-friendly interface. Its service aspect involves the technical support that comes with the product, as well as the music download service offered through iTunes. The brand aspect is defined by the Apple and iPod brands, which differentiate this offering from other functionally similar offerings, such as those by Microsoft, Dell, and Sony. The price reflects the retail price at which the iPod is being sold to customers. Incentives include monetary rewards such as price reductions, coupons, and educational discounts, as well as non-monetary rewards such as free music and video downloads.

The communication aspect of the iPod involves activities aiming to inform target customers about the benefits of the iPod and the iTunes service, enhance the iPod and Apple brands, and inform customers about the price of the iPod and the relevant incentives. This information is conveyed to target customers through various media formats such as advertising, public relations, and personal selling, as well as product placement in newscasts, movies, and talk shows.

The distribution aspect of the iPod tactics involves the channels used to deliver the various aspects of the offering to end-users. Thus, the iPod is delivered through multiple direct and indirect channels such as Apple's online store, Apple's brick-and-mortar retail stores, and other retailers such as Best Buy and Circuit City. The music download service is delivered through Apple's iTunes website, and diagnostic and repair service is delivered though Apple's brick-and-mortar stores, as well as through various Apple resellers. The Apple brand is delivered through Apple's website and its brick-and-mortar retail stores, which enable customers to physically experience Apple and iPod brands. The price is delivered through the retailers who collect payments from customers and, when necessary, make adjustments to payments made (e.g., price-matching adjustments and refunds). Finally, incentives are delivered through channels such as print media (e.g., coupons), retail outlets (e.g., price discounts), and the iTunes website (e.g., free music downloads).

The key aspects of tactical analysis are outlined in more detail below.

▸ Product and Service

The key product and service decisions involve factors such as: form (size, shape, and physical structure), features (discrete characteristics of product/service functionality), performance (the level at which the product/service performs on relevant attributes), consistency (the degree to which all individual products and services are identical and consistent with specifications), durability (the expected length of a product's lifecycle), reliability (the probability that the product/service will operate according to its specifications and will not malfunction for the duration of its projected lifecycle), compatibility (the degree to which the product/service is consistent with certain pre-existing standards), style (the product's look and feel), technological design (the technology used to create the product as well as the technology used by the product), packaging (the product container), and ease-of-use (the ease of setting up, using, and disposing of the product).

▸ Brand

A brand is the identity associated with a given entity, which can involve an individual, an offering, a set of offerings, an organization, a country, or even an idea. A brand has two key aspects: (1) *brand identity*, which includes its identifying characteristics such as name, term, sign, symbol, character, and/or design; and (2) *brand meaning,* which reflects a set of offering-related associations in the mind of the buyer. To illustrate, the identity of BMW is captured by elements such as its name and logo, whereas its meaning – the ultimate driving machine – reflects the mental associations customers make with the brand.

The primary function of brand identity is to identify the company's offering and differentiate it from competitors' offerings. In contrast, the primary function of brand meaning is to create value that goes beyond the product and service characteristics of the offering. The brand identity is a fairly objective characteristic of the offering that exists independently of its target customers; in contrast, the brand meaning is subjective in nature and exists primarily in customers' minds.

○ *Brand identity* is typically achieved through attributes such as brand name, logo, symbol, character, slogan, jingle, product design, and packaging. The key criteria for deciding on brand-identity elements are that they should be (1) unique, (2) memorable, (3) likeable, and (4) consistent with the other brand elements, as well as with the meaning of the brand. Brand elements should also be flexible and be able to adapt to changes in the market environment (e.g., to accommodate shifts in consumer preferences) and the company's product line (e.g., to be extendable to other product categories). In addition, the company should be able to protect the uniqueness of its brand elements against infringement on the part of competitors.

○ *Brand meaning* reflects the brand-related perceptions and beliefs, in addition to customers' understanding of this brand's value proposition. The meaning of the brand has dual impact on customers' perceptions of value: (1) it signals the quality of the products and services associated with the brand and (2) it adds value above and beyond the one provided by the underlying product or service. This added value can involve factors such as emotional benefits (e.g., the satisfaction obtained from brand ownership), social benefits (e.g., group acceptance resulting from ownership of a particular brand), and self-expressive benefits (e.g., using the brand as means to express one's identity).

▸ Price

The price reflects the monetary aspect of the offering. It refers to the amount of money the company charges for the benefits provided by its offering. Setting and managing an offering's price is one of the key factors in determining the value of the offering to the company. Indeed, of all marketing mix variables, price is the only one that generates revenue for the company; all the others are costs. Therefore, companies tend to pay very close attention to price management.

Companies vary in benchmarks they use to determine an offering's price. The four popular approaches to pricing are: cost-based pricing, competitive-parity pricing, customer-value pricing, and market-value pricing.

○ *Cost-based pricing* relies on the company's costs to set the offering's price. In the most extreme case, referred to as *cost-plus pricing* (or markup pricing), the offering's final price is determined by adding a fixed mark-up to the cost of the product or service.

○ *Competitive-parity pricing* involves setting the offering's price in a way that puts this offering's value at parity with that of competitors.

○ *Demand pricing* focuses on customer demand, determined by the customers' willingness to pay for the benefits afforded by the company's offering.

o *Market-value pricing* combines the above three approaches to set a price that is optimal to customers and the company in a competitive context.

The key to determining the optimal price is to consider its implications on the offering's value to customers, collaborators, and the company in a broader context that involves all other aspects of the company's strategy and tactics. Setting the price is really a decision about value, not just price. Thus, the "optimal" price is a price that, in combination with the other marketing mix variables (product, service, brand, incentives, communications, and distribution), delivers superior value to target customers, the company, and collaborators.

▸ Incentives

Incentives offer solutions, typically short-term, aimed at enhancing the value of the offering by providing additional benefits and/or reducing costs. Most incentives can be divided into one of two categories: incentives given to customers and incentives given to channel members (also referred to as trade incentives).

o *Customer incentives.* Based on the type of reward, customer incentives can be divided into two groups: monetary and non-monetary. The most common forms of monetary incentives are coupons, rebates, price reductions, and volume discounts. The most common forms of non-monetary incentives are premiums, prizes, contests, sweepstakes, games, and loyalty programs. In contrast to monetary incentives, which typically aim to reduce an offering's costs, non-monetary incentives typically aim to enhance the offering's benefits.

o *Channel (trade) incentives.* Similar to customer incentives, trade incentives can be divided into two main types: monetary and non-monetary. Monetary incentives involve payments or price discounts given as encouragement to purchase the product or as an inducement to promote the product to customers. Typical monetary trade incentives include slotting allowances (incentives paid to a distributor to allocate shelf space for a new product), stocking allowances (incentives paid to a distributor to carry extra inventory in anticipation of an increase in demand), cooperative advertising allowances (incentives paid by the manufacturer to a distributor in return for featuring its products or services in a retailer's advertisements), display allowances (incentives paid by the manufacturer to a distributor in return for prominently displaying its products), and volume discounts (price reductions based on purchase volume). Non-monetary trade incentives designed to encourage channel support for the company's offering typically include contests (e.g., vacation trips, cars, and other awards given to the best achievers), bonus merchandise (free goods offered as a reward for purchasing a particular item), and buy-back guarantees (an agreement that the manufacturer will buy back from the distributor product quantities not sold in a certain timeframe).

▸ Communications

The communication aspect of the marketing mix involves the process of informing the target audience (customers as well as collaborators) about the benefits of the company's offering. Managing the communication aspect of an offering involves six key decisions: setting a goal, developing a message, determining the budget, identifying the media, developing the creative solution, implementing the communication campaign, and evaluating the results. The key aspects of these decisions are outlined in more detail below.

o *Goal.* The goal identifies a set of criteria to be achieved by the communication campaign within a given timeframe. The three most common communication goals involve (1) creating and/or raising *awareness* of the offering, (2) creating and/or strengthening buyer *preferences* for the offering, and (3) inducing an *action* (e.g., purchase the offering, contact the company for information).

o *Message.* The message identifies the information to be communicated to target customers. The message can involve any of the five value-creation marketing mix variables: product, service, brand, price, and incentives. To illustrate, a company can choose to promote the benefits of its product and service, communicate the meaning of its brand, publicize its price, and inform customers about its current incentives.

o *Budget.* There are several different approaches to determine the total communication budget: (1) the *goal-driven* approach is based on an estimate of the resources required to achieve the company's strategic goal, (2) the *percentage-of-sales* approach implies setting the budget as a fraction of the company's sales revenues, (3) the *competitive-parity* approach implies setting the budget at par with competitors, (4) the *legacy* approach implies setting the budget based on the prior year's expenditures, and (5) the *affordability* approach implies setting the budget based on resources available for promotional activities. In general, the goal-driven approach tends to dominate the others in its ability to estimate more effectively the resources required to achieve the company's communication goals. The competitive-parity and percentage-of-sales approaches can provide further insights into the budgeting decision. The legacy and affordability approaches are the least likely to provide an accurate budget estimate.

o *Media.* The media type involves the means used by the company to convey its message. Most popular media types include advertising (e.g., television, radio, print, online, outdoor, and point-of-purchase), public relations, direct marketing, personal selling, event sponsorship, and product placement. In addition to deciding on the allocation of resources across different types of media, media decisions involve deciding on the specific media channels within each of the media types. To illustrate, within the domain of television advertising, the media channel decision involves selecting particular shows and time slots in which the company's message will be best positioned to reach and influence its target customers. To illustrate, beer companies often choose to advertise during popular sport events with a predominantly male audience, whereas beauty products are typically advertised during shows with a predominantly female audience.

o *Creative.* The creative solution involves translating the company's message into the language of the selected media format (e.g., television, print, or radio). The creative solution involves factors such as copy text (e.g., wording of the headline and the body text), presentation format (e.g., product demonstrations, celebrity endorsements, and slice-of-life stories), and visual elements (e.g., pictures, photos, and graphics).

○ *Implementation.* The implementation aspect of marketing communications identifies the timeline and the logistics of executing the message, media, and creative decisions. Implementation has two key aspects: the processes involved in executing the message, media, and creative strategy (e.g., producing the ad and placing it in the appropriate media channel), and the people managing these processes.

○ *Control.* The control aspect of marketing communications involves evaluating the success of the communication campaign. The most commonly used criteria for success involve measuring the following five factors: (1) comprehension (the degree to which the target audience understands the message embedded in the advertisement), (2) recall (the degree to which an advertisement is remembered by the target audience), (3) persuasion (the advertisement's ability to strengthen buyers' preferences for the product), (4) purchase intent (an advertisement's ability to create a mental disposition in the consumer to buy the offering), and (5) sales (i.e., the degree to which the advertisement influences a product's sales).

When deciding on which particular method to use, it is important to note that none of these measures is a universal indicator of advertising effectiveness. The key to deciding which metric to use is determined by the goal of the campaign. Thus, if the goal is to create awareness (e.g., in the case of a new product introduction), then comprehension, and/or recall should be measured; if the goal is to strengthen preferences, then the persuasiveness of the advertisement should be measured; if the goal is to incite action, then behavior should be measured.

▸ Distribution

The value-delivery aspect of the marketing mix captures the channel through which the offering is delivered to customers, collaborators, and the company. The process of designing and managing distribution channels involves several key decisions: channel structure, channel ownership, channel type, and channel coverage.

○ *Channel structure.* Based on their structure, there are three basic types of value-delivery models: direct, indirect, and hybrid. Direct distribution involves a business model in which the manufacturer and the end-customer interact directly with each other without intermediaries. Indirect distribution involves a business model in which the manufacturer and the end-customer interact with each other through intermediaries, such as wholesalers and retailers. Hybrid distribution involves a business model in which the manufacturer and the end-customer interact with each other through multiple channels – for example, directly and through intermediaries such as wholesalers and/or retailers.

○ *Channel ownership.* Conventional marketing channels comprise independent companies (e.g., manufacturers, wholesalers, and retailers) each maximizing their own profitability. Because the profitability of the channel as a whole can be increased by coordinating the activities of each of its individual members, there is an increasing trend toward channel coordination. The coordination could be (1) ownership-based, in which different channel members are parts of the same company, (2) contractual, in which coordination is achieved through binding contractual agreements between channel members (e.g., long-term contractual agreements, joint ventures, and franchise agreements), and (3) implicit, in which channel coordination is achieved without explicit contractual agreements.

○ *Channel type*. Channels vary in terms of the breadth and depth of their assortments. Based on the *breadth* of the assortment of items carried by a distributor, channels can be classified into one of two categories: specialized and broad. Specialized distributors, such as Office Depot, CarMax, and Toys "R" Us, tend to carry relatively narrow assortments; in contrast, non-specialized distributors, such as Wal-Mart, Costco, and Carrefour, tend to carry much more extensive assortments. Based on the *depth* of assortment of items carried by a distributor, channels can be classified into one of two categories: limited and extensive. Limited-assortment distributors, such as 7-Eleven and Circle K, carry a relatively small number of items, whereas extensive-assortment distributors, such as Home Depot and Wal-Mart, stock a fairly large number of items.

○ *Channel coverage*. Distribution strategies vary in the degree to which they can make an offering available to customers in a given market (e.g., the number of outlets at which offerings are made available to target customers). In this context, *extensive distribution* implies that an offering is (or will be) readily accessible by a fairly large proportion of customers in a given market, whereas *limited distribution* implies that the accessibility of the offering is fairly limited (e.g., the offering is available only through specialized retailers).

Using the Action-Planning Framework in Case Analysis

Most cases involve decisions concerning the tactical aspects of an offering, such as whether to add a particular feature to a given product or service, whether and how to brand an offering, how to set the price, how to promote the offering, and how to set up distribution channels. The basic principle following from the G-S-T-I-C framework is that in order to decide on a specific tactical issue, one first needs to identify (1) the *goal* the company is trying to achieve with this offering, (2) the relevant aspects of its *strategy* (i.e., target customers, competitors, collaborators, company resources, and context factors), as well as (3) the other relevant *tactics* of the offering (i.e., product, service, branding, pricing, incentives, communication, and distribution).

To illustrate, consider the following case: Your client is launching a new product and has asked your advice to determine its pricing. How would you approach this problem?

The first step in solving this case is to identify the *goal* the company is trying to achieve. Identifying the company's goal is important because its pricing strategy is often a function of the goal. To illustrate, a company is likely to set lower prices when its goal is to rapidly penetrate the market and gain market share than when it has the goal of increasing profit margins.

The next step is to identify the *strategy* and analyze its impact on the pricing decision. Strategy analysis involves the following five factors, illustrated in Figure 4:

Figure 4. Strategic Factors in Price Setting

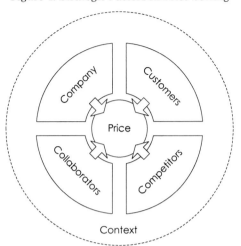

- *Customer factors.* An offering's pricing strategy is a function of customers' willingness to pay for the benefits it offers. Greater benefits lead to greater willingness to pay for the offering. In this context, customers' price sensitivity can determine the quantity sold at different price levels. Pricing based entirely on customers' willingness to pay is often referred to as demand pricing.

- *Company factors.* Pricing is a function of the strategic assets and core competencies of the company, which determine its cost structure. To illustrate, lower cost structure provides the company with the strategic option to lower its price without incurring a loss. Pricing based entirely on the company's costs is often referred to as cost-based pricing.

- *Collaborator factors.* Pricing is also a function of the goals and resources of company collaborators (e.g., channel partners). To illustrate, the price of offerings sold though consolidated distribution channels such as Wal-Mart, is likely to be influenced to a great degree by the pricing strategies of these channels.

- *Competitive factors.* Prices of competitive offerings have a direct impact on an offering's price. To illustrate, based on its strategic goals, a company can set the price of its offering at par, below, or above that of competitors. Pricing based entirely on competitors' prices is often referred to as competitive-parity pricing.

- *Context factors.* Pricing is also a function of various social, economic, political, technological, and regulatory factors describing the environment in which the company operates. To illustrate, the price of travel services is influenced by seasons (e.g., summer vs. winter travel), the price of high-tech products is a function of the availability of superior technologies, and the price of gasoline, tobacco, and alcohol products is a function of government regulations and taxation.

The third step in setting a price involves identifying the *tactics* (the other marketing mix factors) and their impact on the offering's price (Figure 5).

Figure 5. Tactical Factors in Price Setting

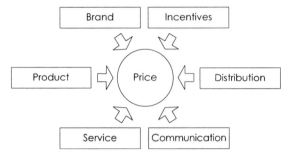

- ○ *Product and service.* Product and service characteristics of the offering are key drivers of an offering's price. Thus, the price is a function of the monetary value target customers are willing to pay for the benefits provided by the company's products and services. Typically, a company can set higher prices for highly differentiated products and services than for commoditized offerings.

- ○ *Brand.* An offering's brand can also have a significant impact on pricing. To illustrate, strong brands command substantial price premiums over weaker brands and non-branded offerings. In fact, the price premium associated with a given brand is often used to measure the strength of this brand.

- ○ *Incentives.* Incentives are typically used to make further adjustments to the offering's price in a way that better meets the needs of target customers, collaborators, and the company. Incentives, and in particular monetary incentives, have become an integral component of a company's pricing strategy, such that an offering's price is typically augmented by some form of a monetary incentive offered to channel members (e.g., volume discounts and promotional allowances) and customers (e.g., price reductions and coupons).

- ○ *Communications.* Pricing decisions can be influenced by the offering's communication strategy, as well. To illustrate, an offering might be priced 50% less than the market leader to more effectively communicate its benefits (e.g., "half the price").

- ○ *Distribution.* An offering's price is likely to be a function of multiple factors, such as channel structure, channel ownership, channel type, and channel coverage. To illustrate, a company selling though indirect channels typically cannot directly set retail prices; instead, it suggests the price at which the offering should be sold to customers (e.g., manufacturer's suggested retail price, or MSRP).

Action-Planning Case Examples

Differentiating a Commodity Product (Cereal Case)

Interviewer: Our firm has recently been approached by a major cereal manufacturer who wants to launch a new cereal. What recommendations would you make to this client to help differentiate its product?

You: Well, I would start by asking the client who the target customers for the new cereal are.

Interviewer: 4-12 year olds.

You: Great. In this case, we should probably consider two customer segments: 4-12 year olds, who are the end-users of the cereal, and their parents, who will decide which cereal to buy and will actually purchase the cereal. This means that the new cereal should be appealing to children so that they want the product but should also have benefits that make parents feel good about purchasing it for their kids.

Interviewer: Good. How do we do this?

You: Do we know what kinds of benefits in a cereal are important for these two groups?

Interviewer: What do you think?

You: Let's start with parents. Parents are likely to look for a cereal that is both healthy and appealing to their children. Do we know anything about this cereal's nutritional value?

Interviewer: Not much. Do you have any suggestions?

You: Well, one option is to develop a cereal that is organic. It could also be low in sugar – for example, by using sugar-substitute sweeteners, such as Splenda. Thus, the product can be a healthy alternative to high-sugar, artificially flavored children's cereal.

Interviewer: Good. What's next?

You: In addition to being attractive to parents, the cereal needs to appeal to kids, who often influence parents' buying decisions. Do we know what makes a cereal attractive to children?

Interviewer: No, this is part of the assignment.

You: I actually do not have an in-depth knowledge of children's cereal preferences. When it comes to adult's cereal preferences, important attributes are taste, shape, and texture. So, I presume children will enjoy these attributes as well. My guess is that for children it is also important that the cereal is fun and enjoyable to eat.

Interviewer: And how would you suggest that the client makes the cereal fun to eat?

You: One way is to associate the cereal with something fun, such as a character, or a name that children would remember. In fact, since cereal is essentially a commodity product, branding would be essential in differentiating it from competitor's goods. Does the client have any ideas about how it wants to brand the cereal?

Interviewer: No, this is also part of the assignment.

You: Since the cereal should appeal to both parents and children, the brand image should also be consistent with the needs of these two segments. Because most of the nutritional information is readily available on the package, I would say that making the brand appealing to children should be our primary goal.

Interviewer: How do you propose the client creates such a brand?

You: Well, the key decisions to consider are developing a brand identity and an image in order to position the cereal. This can be done through developing a name, a character, and a slogan.

Interviewer: Can you come up with a name for me?

You: Sure. I think having a play on words or an alliteration may be a good idea, for instance, as in Cap'n Crunch, or Frosted Flakes. So maybe a name like...Kangaroo Krisp would work.

Interviewer: Sounds good. Tell me more about the character. Why would you need one?

You: A character is an important component for branding a commodity regardless of industry. The Michelin Man and the Green Giant differentiate otherwise indistinguishable products such as tires and frozen vegetables. The first thing that comes to mind when you think of Frosted Flakes, for instance, is Tony the Tiger.

Interviewer: Fine. So what kind of character would fit this cereal?

You: The character should be appealing for both children and parents, while adequately representing the strengths of the product. An exciting and fun character would help kids remember the brand. I recall that in the early '90s, Captain Planet was a popular environmentalist superhero. Maybe modeling a character after him would give kids the sense of fun and excitement that they want while displaying to parents that this is an organic product.

Interviewer: OK. By the way, earlier you suggested that the cereal should be named Kangaroo Krisp. Do you think this name fits with the superhero character?

You: That is a very good point. It is very important that the brand name and the character are consistent. So, in this case we should have a superhero kangaroo? (laughs) In any case this is just an initial suggestion to illustrate the general idea. I would recommend that the client hire a firm specializing in identifying brand names that best convey the meaning we would like it to convey.

Interviewer: Anything else you think that the client should consider?

You: It is also important to determine the price at which the cereal would be sold. Does the client have a preconceived idea of how to price the cereal?

Interviewer: Nothing specific. However, because it is organic, the cereal will be sold at a price that is 10% to 20% higher than its non-organic competition.

You: Well, a higher price might turn some customers off. Do we know anything about customers' price sensitivity?

Interviewer: What do you think?

You: Most likely customers will vary in their sensitivity to price; some will be more price-sensitive, whereas others will care more about the quality of the cereal they purchase for their children than about price.

Interviewer: Let's focus on buyers that are not very price sensitive, and care more about quality.

You: In this case, a 20% higher price should not be an issue. In fact, if the cereal is substantially differentiated, the client could explore pricing it even higher. Given that pricing is a key decision, I would recommend that once the cereal has been formulated and the brand developed, they do additional research to identify the best price at which the cereal should be sold.

Interviewer: Good. Earlier you mentioned that we should consider incentives. Can you elaborate?

You: Sure. Like the other aspects of this cereal, the client should develop incentives that appeal to both children and their parents. Something a lot of children look for when they are buying a cereal with their parents is some kind of toy or game that comes with the package. As for parents, even though you mentioned earlier that they were not very price sensitive, offering coupons can be a great way to appeal to customers who do care more about price.

Interviewer: Anything else?

You: We also need to develop a communication campaign and a distribution strategy for the cereal.

Interviewer: So how would you do that?

You: Well, following the strategy of appealing to both children and parents, any advertising campaign the client develops should make sure to target both age groups. Thus, ads for the cereal should be included in media that is targeted towards the parents of young children such as, "Good Mother Magazine," while also targeting children through TV commercials during cartoons and children's programs.

Interviewer: Where do you think they should sell the product?

You: Where does the client currently sell its other cereals?

Interviewer: Mainly grocery stores and supermarkets.

You: Both of these are viable channels for the new cereal. Given that the primary buyers of the cereal are health-conscious individuals, specialty organic stores and health centers might also be good places to sell the cereal.

Interviewer: Sounds good. Do you have any questions for us?

CASE COMMENTS: The case raises the issue of how to differentiate a commodity-like product such as cereal. The interviewee relies on the C-C-D framework (creating-communicating-delivering value) to identify the key factors that can be used to differentiate an offering: product, brand, price, incentives, communication, and distribution. In this case it is crucial to realize that although the cereal is targeted to children, parents are the actual buyers of the cereal and their preferences should also be considered as an integral part of the product development process. Note also that in this case the interviewer often answers a question with a question, in which case the interviewee identifies the possible scenarios and then explores them one by one.

Adding a New Product Feature (Water Filter Case)

Interviewer: Our client is a major competitor in the market for pitcher water filtration systems. Currently, their pitcher retails for $30 – at a cost to the company of $10 and with retail margins of 25%. The client is considering adding a new built-in indicator on the pitcher to help the consumer know when to change filters, at an additional cost to the company of $7.45 per pitcher. Is this a good idea?

You: You mentioned retail margins. Are there any other intermediaries, such as wholesalers?

Interviewer: Good question. Assume that we only have to consider retail margins.

You: Well, let's start by doing a simple calculation of the reduction of profit on each pitcher because of the increased cost to produce it. With retail margins of 25%, the revenue that the client receives on each pitcher is $30 \cdot 75\% = \$22.50$. Without the built-in indicator, the profit on each pitcher is roughly $22.50 - $10 = $12.50. With the added cost of a filter usage indicator, the profit on each pitcher would be $22.50 - $17.45 = $5.05. This means a reduction of profits for the company of 7.45/12.50 for each pitcher, or an overall reduction of 60% for profits on pitchers. That's a substantial decline in profits.

Interviewer: So what should the company do?

You: My first impression is to say that such a large reduction of profits for the client is a bad idea. But I want to understand the problem a little more before I make any suggestions. What are the company's goals with regard to these indicators?

Interviewer: The client is hoping to increase sales revenues.

You: As I understand it, there are two components to these pitcher water filtration systems: a pitcher, and a filter. Do we know how much the filters sell for and what the retail margins are like?

Interviewer: A pack of 3 filters sells for $16.90 and has a retail margin of 25%. The cost to the company for a pack of 3 filters is $6.95.

You: And how do these filters work? How often should they be changed?

Interviewer: The suggested usage time for a filter is one month.

You: So with retail margins of 25%, the company's sales per set of three filters is $16.90 \cdot 75\% = \$12.68$, and at a cost of $6.95, the profits for the company are $12.68 - $6.95 = $5.73. This means that ideally over a year the company would make profits of $5.73 \cdot 4 = \$22.92$ on filters.

Interviewer: So how would you calculate the sales revenues?

You: Sales revenues in this case are equal to:

(#users · pitcher price) + (#users · filter price · usage rate of filters)

Interviewer: So what does that mean in terms of the client's question?

You: It means that the usage rate of filters may play a pivotal role in the client's profitability. Do we know how many filters the average customer uses per year?

Interviewer: Yes, given the number of pitchers sold, the company estimates that consumers on average buy 9 filters a year.

You: That means that at 9 filters a year, the client's profit on a 3-pack of filters is $5.73, times 3, or $17.19. The company suggests that the filter be changed approximately every month, which would mean an additional 3 pack per year or an increase in profits of $5.73 per year for each pitcher sold. This assumes, of course, that in the presence of a usage indicator, people will modify their filter replacement rate to change filters every month.

Interviewer: Okay, so what does that mean in terms of the client's question?

You: Well, the question now, is whether the increase in sales as a result of increased frequency of filter changes outweighs the increase in costs from the new indicator on pitchers. The increased cost of the indicator is $7.45, while the increase in revenues per year that are expected as a result of the indicator are as high as $5.73. This means that within less than two years the client could break even in terms of the added cost of the indicator. Since you said that pitchers typically lasted several years, this would mean that profits would increase in the long run as a result of these new pitchers with indicators.

Interviewer: So does that mean you agree that this is a good idea?

You: Well, just to put this into perspective, looking back at the revenue equation:

(#users · pitcher price) + (#users · filter price · usage rate of filters)

Suppose the client acquires a million customers; the revenue without indicators for a 2-year span would be:

1 million · $22.50 + 2 · (1 million · $12.68 · 3) = $98,580,000

With indicators, however, the revenue over that same time period would be:

1 million · $22.50 + 2 · (1 million · $12.68 · 4) = $123,940,000

This is a difference of $25,360,000. Meanwhile, the added cost to the company for the indicator over that same 2-year time period would be:

$$1 \text{ million} \cdot \$7.45 = \$7,450,000.$$

Therefore, adding the indicator will have a positive net effect on company's profits, equal to $25,360,000 - $7,450,000 = $18,910,000.

Interviewer: So what do these numbers mean?

You: It seems as though even a small alteration in the frequency of changing filters results in a large change in revenues, and thus profits, in the long run. Therefore, adding an indicator on pitchers is a good idea, even though it may at first appear to result in a loss if you don't take into account its impact on filter usage rates.

Interviewer: Good. Thanks for coming in. Enjoy the rest of your day.

CASE COMMENTS: This case is about understanding the importance of managing product usage on a company's bottom line. At first glance, adding filter indicators to pitchers seems like a substantial and unnecessary reduction in profits. However, the interviewee realizes that usage rate actually plays a very important role in sales. In fact, even a small alteration in the frequency of changing filters results in a large change in revenues and thus profits in the long run. This outweighs the initial cost of adding indicators to pitchers. Hence, the interviewee recommends that the company go ahead with the project.

Product Pricing (Eye Drops Case)

Interviewer: One of our clients recently developed new eye drops that, when applied every morning, eliminate nearsightedness in 30% of cases. What should the client consider when determining the price of the product, and what price would you suggest?

You: Well, that's an interesting situation. There are several methods for approaching the pricing of a new product. One important aspect is the prices of substitute products.

Interviewer: Can you give me some examples of this?

You: Sure, I use corrective eyewear myself. I used to wear glasses, which cost about $180 and lasted for 2 years, for a cost of $90 a year. Now I wear contact lenses, and a year's supply costs me about $120. Since both of these are substitutes for the new corrective eye drops, the product can justifiably be priced in the $90-$120 price range. If it turns out that these eye drops are easy to use and more convenient for customers than the alternatives, then the product can be sold at a premium, say $140 or $150.

Interviewer: Is that your suggested price?

You: Not quite, that examines only the competitive aspect of pricing. It is very important to consider other factors, as well, such as the overall demand for this product.

Interviewer: How would you do that?

You: Well, do we know approximately what percentage of people use corrective eyewear?

Interviewer: We believe it's somewhere around 50%.

You: And of that 50%, I'm guessing the majority are nearsighted?

Interviewer: That's right. We believe that around 70% of corrective eyewear users are nearsighted.

You: And how many units of eye drops would the customer need to buy a year?

Interviewer: For simplicity, let's say that the product is sold in a yearly supply.

You: Sure. You mentioned earlier that the client estimated a 30% success rate for the product. Do we know how much of the nearsighted population is expected to try the new product, and what the product adoption rate should be?

Interviewer: Let's say marketing research estimates that approximately 25% of the nearsighted population will try the new product, and approximately 50% of successful cases actually adopt the product.

You:	Great. So 25% of target customers will try the product, with a 30% success rate, and of those, 50% adopt the product. Assuming that the U.S. population is about 300 million, times 50% that use corrective eyewear, times 70% that are nearsighted, times 25% product trial, times a 30% success rate, times an approximate 50% adoption rate, this gives us an estimated demand of...give me a second...about 4 million customers.
Interviewer:	So what does that tell us?
You:	Well, we can use that information to approach pricing in terms of the needs of the company, or in other words the minimum price that the company should charge in order to break even. Do we know what the fixed costs of the product have been for the client, or at least how much money has gone into R&D?
Interviewer:	The client approximates that as much as $500 million went into the development of this product.
You:	And do we know the variable cost of producing a year's supply of eye drops?
Interviewer:	Let's say it's about $15.
You:	With that information we can say that the total cost for the client is approximately $560 million (4 million customers multiplied by $15 annual variable cost plus the initial fixed costs of $500 million). This means that in order for the client to break even in its first year, the manufacturer's price should be at least $560 million divided by 4 million, or about $140. What kind of trade margins can we expect the client's collaborators to demand?
Interviewer:	Let's say retail margins are about 20%.
You:	Should I assume that this is based on the retailer's selling price rather than on the price they purchase it from the manufacturer?
Interviewer:	Yes.
You:	So, with those kinds of margins, the product should be sold to customers at a price of at least $175 ($140/80%).
Interviewer:	Is that your suggested price?
You:	Not necessarily. These calculations assume that the company's primary goal is to break even within a year, which might not be the case. What we know for sure is that if the company intends to make money on this product, its retail price should not be below its costs – $18.75 ($15 annual variable costs/80% manufacturer margin).
Interviewer:	Great. What else would you consider?
You:	Another important issue to consider is customers' willingness to pay for the product. This will essentially entail employing different research methods, such as surveys and conjoint analysis, to determine

how much customers are willing to spend on this product. In the absence of proprietary data, we could use as a benchmark the price of competitive products, which we determined to be around $140-$150.

Interviewer: So what would you say to the client in terms of the original question?

You: Well, the client should analyze substitute products to get an idea of what competitive prices in the market look like. Beyond this, the client should definitely take into account its cost structure, its profit goals, and the estimated demand. With this information the client can estimate a price range for its product, which, from our conversation earlier, could be around $150.

Interviewer: Great. And that said, there's another interview scheduled. Thanks for coming in. We'll give you a call later this week.

CASE COMMENTS: This case presents a typical new-product pricing problem. To identify the optimal price, the interviewee utilizes three different methods. The first method suggests a price based on substitute offerings such as glasses and contact lenses. The second method estimates product demand and fixed and variable costs in order to determine the minimum price at which the client company would break even. The third method suggests a price based on customers' willingness to pay. The final price incorporates the results derived from all three methods.

Product Pricing (Light Bulb Case)

Interviewer: Your client, General Electric, has developed a new technology that will make possible creating light bulbs that will last 10 times longer than the traditional ones. The cost to bring the new light bulb to market is $500 million. Should GE make this investment? If yes, how should the new light bulb be priced?

You: The basic rule for making the go/no go decision is that the benefits from launching the new product should outweigh the costs. The costs are already given – $500 million. Can I assume that this figure includes all related costs such as opportunity costs, management costs, marketing costs, etc.?

Interviewer: Yes.

You: Okay. Then the question is whether the monetary value of the benefits generated by the new light bulb will exceed $500 million. One way to approach this problem is to calculate the break-even volume of a fixed-cost investment of $500 million and then estimate whether this sales volume is feasible within the given timeframe. The break-even volume of a fixed-cost investment (BEV_{FC}) is the ratio of the size of the fixed-cost investment to the unit margin, which, in turn, is the difference between the unit selling price and unit variable costs.

$$BEV_{FC} = \frac{\text{Fixed-cost investment}}{\text{Unit selling price - Unit variable cost}}$$

Therefore, to evaluate the feasibility of the product launch, we need to know the unit selling price and the unit variable costs. Let's start with the selling price. First, let's estimate customers' willingness to pay for the new light bulb. Because customers are faced with a choice of buying either a traditional or the new long-life light bulb, it is important to understand their cost-benefit tradeoff. Do we know the price and the longevity of GE's traditional light bulbs?

Interviewer: Assume that a regular light bulb is priced at around $2 for a pack of four and lasts 1,200 hours.

You: Okay. Assuming that an average light bulb is used between 3 and 4 hours per day, 1,200 hours will translate into roughly one year of usage. So, GE could market the new light bulb as lasting 10 years. The question then is how much extra a customer would be willing to pay for a light bulb that lasts 10 years if a regular light bulb lasts one year and costs 50 cents. By the way, can I assume that $2 is the retail price?

Interviewer: Yes.

You: Estimating consumers' willingness to pay is a complex question that requires additional research. Here I will assume that to receive the benefit of extended light bulb longevity, consumers will be willing to pay up to three times the price of a regular light bulb. This means $1.50. This, however is the retail price. Next, we need to know the price at which GE sells the light bulb to distributors (the wholesale price).

Interviewer: Assume that retailer margin is 20%

You: Does this include breakage, shipping costs, inventory costs, etc.?

Interviewer: Yes.

You: Does this also include wholesaler margins?

Interviewer: Yes.

You: Okay. This means that GE's unit selling price is $1.50*80% = $1.20. We also need to know the estimated variable costs for manufacturing the new light bulb.

Interviewer: Assume that the variable costs are 30 cents per light bulb.

You: Okay. Now we can calculate the break-even volume as follows:

$$\text{BEV}_{FC} = \frac{\$500 \text{ million}}{\$1.20 - \$.30} \approx 550 \text{ million light bulbs}$$

Next, we need to estimate the likelihood of GE being able to sell 550 million light bulbs within a given time frame. What is GE's time horizon for recouping its initial investment?

Interviewer: Five years.

You: We also need to know how many light bulbs GE sells annually.

Interviewer: GE sells about 600 million standard incandescent bulbs annually.

You: Okay. Let's assume that the diffusion of the new product is such that the sales volume grows by 5% every year. Thus, in five years 25% of all light bulbs sold by GE will be long-lasting ones. This means that within 5 years the sales volume of the new light bulb would be:

(.05 + .10 + .15 + .20 + .25) * 600 million = 450 million light bulbs

Well, based on our assumptions and calculations so far, it does not seem that GE will be able to achieve its financial goals of breaking even within 5 years from the product launch...

Interviewer: So, is it your recommendation that GE does not launch the new light bulb?

You: Well, not necessarily. There are additional issues to consider. First, this break-even analysis involved a number of assumptions. One approach is to perform a sensitivity analysis and examine scenarios using different assumptions to see how sensitive our results are. For example, we assumed that customers will be willing to pay up to three times the price of a regular light bulb for the long-lasting light bulb. If market research data show that customers are willing to pay four rather than three times more, then the break-even volume would be 385 million, which will support bringing the new light bulb to market. There are other issues to consider as well...

Interviewer: Such as?

You: So far we have only considered the direct monetary impact of the new light bulb on GE's bottom line. It is also important to consider potential non-monetary factors such as possible synergies with other products. For example, can the technology used for the new light bulb be applied to other projects? Would the development of the new light bulb enable GE to develop know-how that could potentially enhance its existing core competencies or even result in new ones? To what degree would introducing the new light bulb enhance GE's image as a leader in technology and innovation, and how will this influence GE's ability to attract top engineering talent?

Interviewer: Good. Is there anything else that GE should consider?

You: Definitely. So far we assumed that GE's new product has no competitors. Does GE have a patent on this invention?

Interviewer: Yes, but this does not guarantee that competitors such as Sylvania or Phillips cannot come up with alternative technology that produces a long-lasting light bulb similar to GE's.

You: Right. In the absence of competitors, it is likely that GE's long-lasting light bulb will steal share from some of its competitors in the traditional light bulb market. This means that the 5% annual growth could be calculated using the entire light bulb market rather than only GE's sales. If GE's existing competitors introduce similar long-lasting products, then one can assume that the new products will draw sales proportionate to their current market share, in which case our calculations using GE's current sales as a base are correct. Do we know GE's share of the traditional light bulb market?

Interviewer: Let's say it is around 20%

You: In this case, one could argue that in the absence of competition, we should use the entire light bulb market of 5 * 600 million = 3 billion as the basis for calculating the size of the market for the new light bulb. This would imply that, in the absence of competition, within five years the market size would be $3 billion. This number is more than five times larger than the 550 million light bulbs that GE needs to sell in order to break even.

Interviewer: Fine. Anything else?

You: I think it would also be very important to examine how the introduction of the new light bulb will impact the sales of GE's existing light
bulb product line. Would the new light bulb be branded with GE's
name?

Interviewer: Most likely.

You: In that case the sales of the new light bulb will inevitably cannibalize the sales of GE's traditional light bulbs, especially if both the
long-lasting and the traditional light bulbs are branded with GE's
name. It is, therefore, imperative to estimate the magnitude and the
financial impact of such cannibalization.

Interviewer: And how would you do that?

You: One approach is to estimate the break-even rate of cannibalization,
which indicates the maximum proportion of sales volume of the new
offering that could come from the company's existing offering(s)
without incurring a loss. To calculate this I would need additional
data. Do we know the variable costs associated with GE's traditional
light bulbs?

Interviewer: Assume that they are 15 cents.

You: Okay. The break-even rate of cannibalization can generally be calculated as follows:

$$BER_C = \frac{\text{Margin}_{\text{NewOffering}}}{\text{Margin}_{\text{OldOffering}}} = \frac{(\text{Price - Variable cost})_{\text{NewOffering}}}{(\text{Price - Variable cost})_{\text{OldOffering}}}$$

This formula, however, assumes that the purchase rate of both
products is identical. Unlike traditional light bulbs, which are re-
placed every year, in our case a customer purchasing the new long-
lasting light bulb would not repurchase the light bulb in the next 10
years. A back-of-the-envelope approach to account for this difference
in the repurchase rates is to disperse the revenues from the sales of
the new light bulb over 10 years. In this case,

$$BER_C = \frac{\text{Margin}_{\text{NewOffering}}}{10 \cdot \text{Margin}_{\text{OldOffering}}} = \frac{\$1.20 - \$.30}{10 \cdot (\$.50 \cdot 80\% - \$.15)} = 36\%$$

This means that in order to be profitable the new light bulb should
cannibalize no more than 36% of GE's sales of traditional light
bulbs, which in turn implies that at least 64% of sales should come
from competitive offerings.

Interviewer: Is this realistic?

You: Well, if GE's current share is 20% and none of its competitors have
introduced a similar long-life light bulb it is likely that the new light
bulb market should draw share from the existing companies in proportion to their current shares. This implies that the cannibalization

rate of GE's own traditional light bulbs should be around 20%. Thus, based on this preliminary analysis, a break-even rate of cannibalization of 36% seems achievable.

Interviewer: Okay. Let's talk about something else. Do you have any questions for us?

CASE COMMENTS: This case combines two problems: a new product launch ("go" – "no go") decision and a pricing decision. The interviewee approaches this problem with a cost-benefit analysis, starting by determining the volume of sales necessary to break even within a given time frame. Although this analysis indicates that GE will not break even in the first 5 years of sales of the new light bulb, the interviewee explores other pros and cons of the new offering. The interviewee considers the nonmonetary impact of the offering, such as possible synergies that would result, as well as the impact of the new light bulb on the product line, both in terms of the shares it would steal from competition as well as from GE's own product line (cannibalization).

Pricing Business-to-Business Products (CRM Software Case)

Interviewer: Our client is a software developer that has recently created a new customer relationship management (CRM) software that allows businesses to automate their entire marketing, sales, and customer service operations. The client has approached us to help determine the appropriate pricing of its software. What suggestions would you give them?

You: Do we know exactly what this software does for its customers?

Interviewer: The software streamlines the process of collecting, storing, and analyzing customer information.

You: And do we know the impact of this software on a company's operations?

Interviewer: The software typically leads to a shorter selling cycle and savings generated by lower sales personnel turnover and a shorter start-up time for new sales representatives. There are other factors as well, but let's focus on these three for now.

You: All right. Let me make sure I understand this correctly. A shorter selling cycle means that it would take less time for a salesperson to make a sale?

Interviewer: Yes.

You: Lower personnel turnover means that salespeople would be more satisfied and will stay longer with the company?

Interviewer: Yes.

You: Finally, a shorter start-up time for new sales representatives means that the newly hired salespeople can be trained faster?

Interviewer: Yes.

You: Generally speaking, the software should be priced such that the benefits from using the software outweigh its costs. The benefits involve the cost reduction from the shorter selling cycle, lower personnel turnover, and savings generated by a shorter start-up time for new sales representatives. The costs involve the costs of buying, implementing, and managing the software.

Interviewer: That might be true but it seems very general. Assume that their client is a financial services company with annual sales of $150 million. How would you go about pricing the software?

You: Let's first consider the benefits, that is, the savings the client will realize as a result of a shorter selling cycle. We need the data on the annual sales expenses and the estimated reduction in its selling cycle as a result of using the new software.

Interviewer: The client estimates that selling costs are 35% of revenues, 15% of which are variable expenses such as sales commission. The estimated reduction in the sales cycle using the new software is an 8-day reduction in a 125-day selling cycle.

You: That would mean that with annual sales of $150 million, the fixed cost of annual sales expense can be calculated as follows:

$$\$150M \cdot (35\% \text{ total selling costs} - 15\% \text{ variable costs}) = \$30M.$$

Interviewer: Okay.

You: And a reduction of 8 days divided by a total selling cycle of 125 times the annual sales expense of $30 million would mean a saving of approximately $1.92 million as a result of a shorter selling cycle.

Interviewer: Okay.

You: Next, we need to estimate the savings generated by a lower turnover. Do we have any additional data?

Interviewer: We have the following information: The customer maintains a sales force of 140 representatives, and has an annual turnover rate of 15%. It takes 50 days of training before a sales representative becomes productive, and the estimated reduction in representative turnover using the new software is 10%.

You: Well, with a sales representative force of 140 and an annual turnover rate of 15%, this means that every year the firm hires 21 new sales representatives.

Interviewer: Okay.

You: As for those 50 days when the sales rep is not yet productive, the daily cost to the client must be the $30 million in annual sales expense we calculated earlier, divided by a sales team of 140 representatives working an approximate 250 work-day year.

$$\text{Salesperson's daily cost} = \frac{\$30M \text{ annual salesforce costs}}{140 \text{ sales reps} \cdot 250 \text{ days per year}} = \$857 \text{ per day}$$

Interviewer: Okay.

You: So, 21 new sales reps per year at a cost of $857 per day for 50 days would equal:

$$21 \cdot \$857 \cdot 50 = \$899,850$$

A 10 percent reduction in turnover would mean that the client would save:

$$\$899,850 \cdot 0.10 = \$89,985$$

Interviewer: Okay.

You: Next, we need to estimate the potential savings generated by a shorter start-up time for new sales representatives. Do we know what the reduction in start-up time for a new salesperson would be using the new software?

Interviewer: It would be about 16 days.

You: This means that the 21 new sales representatives per year, which we calculated earlier, times .9, would now be 19 new sales representatives a year because of the lower turnover. A reduction of 16 days in the start-up time and $857 daily cost of a sales rep means the company would save:

$$16 \cdot 19 \cdot \$857 = \$260,528$$

This means that the total savings for the customer would be:

$1.92M + \$89,985 + \$260,528$, which equals approximately $2.27M.

Interviewer: Are you proposing a price of $2.27 million?

You: Not quite. This number does not take into account the costs incurred by the customer. Do we know what types of costs are usually involved in using such software?

Interviewer: The annual software maintenance and support is $500,000.

You: So the annual savings from this software would be $2.27M - $500,000 = $1.77M.

Interviewer: Are you proposing a price of $1.77 million?

You: Not quite. This number does not take into account the initial cost incurred by the company buying the software. Are there any additional setup costs?

Interviewer: Yes. In addition to the initial purchase price there is an implementation cost.

You: Just to clarify, do implementation costs involve installing the software?

Interviewer: Yes. This is typically done by a third-party firm such as IBM or Bearing Point.

You: And what is the typical cost of installing such software?

Interviewer: Assume that it is about $3 million.

You: The price would also depend on the time the company wants to break even. If we assume a 2-year break-even period, the break-even price is given by the equation:

$$\text{Break-even price} + \$3M = 2 \text{ years} \cdot \$1.77M$$

Hence, the price is $540,000

Interviewer: So, is this how they should price the software?

You: I would consider using a 3-year break-even period, in which case the break-even price would be $2.31 million. Note that this is the break-even price that will make the software revenue-neutral to the client. In order to be able to convince the client to buy the product, we need to make sure that it creates value to the client.

Interviewer: So, what do you propose?

You: Given the 3-year break-even period and the uncertainty involved in implementing new software, we need to offer substantial savings. I would say at least $1 million, maybe more. This will set the upper boundary for the price at $1.31 million.

Interviewer: That's it?

You: Of course we also need to consider two other factors: the cost to develop the software, as well as the price at which competitive software packages are available. Should I address these in more detail?

Interviewer: No need. Good job. Unless you have any other questions for us it's been a pleasure meeting with you, and I hope to talk to you soon.

CASE COMMENTS: This case involves calculating the value of a company's offering to its clients. The interviewee approaches the pricing of the software based on the cost savings from using the software, the costs incurred by buying and implementing the software, as well as the timeframe in which customers are expected to break even. Note that on several occasions the interviewee asks for clarification when the meaning of a particular concept is unclear – not unusual in cases involving industry-specific terminology.

Developing an Advertising Campaign (Energy Drink Case)

Interviewer: You are the CEO of a consumer goods company. How would you go about developing an advertising campaign for a product you are about to launch?

You: First, can you tell me more about the product?

Interviewer: Sure, it is a new, highly-caffeinated energy drink that is supplemented with vitamins, taurine, and other herbal ingredients. It is designed to give its customers a physical and mental boost during periods of strain.

You: Let me start by outlining the general method for developing an advertising campaign. This process can be illustrated using a simple flowchart (drawing the flowchart while naming its key elements).

```
┌─────────────────┐
│      Goal       │
└─────────────────┘
         ⇩
┌─────────────────┐
│     Message     │
└─────────────────┘
         ⇩
┌─────────────────┐
│     Budget      │
└─────────────────┘
         ⇩
┌─────────────────┐
│     Media       │
└─────────────────┘
         ⇩
┌─────────────────┐
│    Creative     │
└─────────────────┘
         ⇩
┌─────────────────┐
│  Implementation │
└─────────────────┘
         ⇩
┌─────────────────┐
│     Control     │
└─────────────────┘
```

Interviewer: Good. Now, walk me through these steps.

You: Sure. First we need to determine the goal the company is trying to achieve with its advertising campaign.

Interviewer: Let's say the company wants to create awareness among its target customers.

You: Do we have any information about the specific level of awareness the company is trying to achieve, as well as a timeframe for achieving it?

Interviewer: Let's say the company wants to achieve 3% awareness in 6 months.

You: Great. The next step is to identify the message to be conveyed by the campaign.

Interviewer: Do you have any suggestions?

You: Well, to develop an effective message, we need to know more about this offering's brand image and its promise to customers.

Interviewer: The name of the drink is Fearless. Its brand image is linked to extreme sports.

You: Well, with that brand image, we can build a message that this drink gives its customers an adrenaline rush such that they are capable of taking on any challenge, no matter how dangerous.

Interviewer: And how much money should the company allocate for its advertising?

You: One way to determine the budget is to calculate the costs associated with achieving the goals of the campaign. Now, you mentioned earlier that the goal is to achieve a level of awareness of 3%. Is this 3% of the target customers or of the entire market?

Interviewer: Assume that you want to create awareness among 3% of the entire U.S. market.

You: Well, in that case, assuming a population of 300 million, this means that we want to create awareness among 9 million people. Do we know the cost of reaching a customer?

Interviewer: Let's say that the CPM – the cost for reaching a thousand customers – is about $20.

You: With a CPM of $20 and a population of 9M, we can expect the budget to be

$$(20 \cdot 9M)/1{,}000 = \$180{,}000.$$

Interviewer: Really? Is that all?

You: You're right, it seems a bit low. One factor we did not take into consideration is the number of impressions needed to create awareness in a given customer. So, let's assume that we need 6 impressions to create awareness. In that case we would expect the budget to be ($180,000 · 6) which is a little over a million.

Interviewer: Fine. How would you suggest that the company spends this money? What media should they use?

You: You mentioned earlier that our client targets customers that participate in extreme sports. I feel like that is a fairly specific group. Some good options that the company can consider are carefully selected television commercial time during extreme sports programming, and event sponsorship of large sporting events. Also the company can sponsor biking, skating, skiing, boarding, surfing, and sky diving competitions.

Interviewer: Great, that is all I need. Unless you have any questions, my secretary can show you to the door. Thanks for coming in today.

CASE COMMENTS: The case calls for identifying the key steps in developing a communication campaign. The interviewee applies a general framework for developing a campaign in order to derive a specific answer to the interviewer's question. Note that in this case the interviewee draws a flowchart to structure the answers.

Managing Distribution (Market Entry Case)

Interviewer: An established European company is considering entering the U.S. market and has sought your advice on whether to distribute its products directly by launching its own stores or to distribute through already existing channels. How would you go about helping them make this decision?

You: Do we know what type of products they are manufacturing?

Interviewer: It is an upscale apparel company.

You: Well, there are three basic types of distribution: direct, indirect, and hybrid. This flowchart can illustrate different distribution models (drawing the flowchart while describing its key elements). Direct distribution involves a business model in which the manufacturer and the end-customer interact directly with each other without intermediaries. In contrast, indirect channels involve one or more intermediaries such as wholesalers and retailers. Finally, a hybrid channel combines both direct and indirect channels.

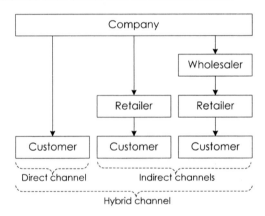

Interviewer: So, what channel would you recommend?

You: Well, the direct distribution model offers better coordination between the manufacturer and the retailer because they are owned by the same entity. Also, it allows for greater cost-efficiency that results from eliminating intermediaries. It also offers closer contact with the end-user, allowing the manufacturer to have first-hand information about customer needs and their reaction to its products.

Interviewer: So it sounds like the company should consider direct distribution?

You: Not necessarily. Establishing direct distribution, especially a brick-and-mortar one, takes time and a large upfront fixed-cost investment. Another issue is that in most cases it is difficult to achieve the same breadth of distribution outlets with direct-distribution as by using multiple intermediaries. Launching and managing a distribution channel requires a different set of core competencies that many manufacturers do not readily have.

Interviewer: So then you would recommend using indirect distribution?

You: Using intermediaries has the advantage of instantly achieving rapid and wide distribution. For example, making the product available in a national chain such as Nordstrom or Neiman-Marcus enables the company to instantly reach the majority of its target customers. Using intermediaries can actually lead to lower distribution costs due to the scale of operations and specialization efficiencies in operations of many retailers. A manufacturer using intermediaries is essentially "renting" rather than buying shelf space for its products; and, as a result, indirect distribution does not require a large upfront investment.

Interviewer: It sounds like using intermediaries is the way to go. Would you have any concerns doing so?

You: Well, using intermediaries introduces another layer of costs to the channel, which might put pressure on the company's margins. Also, an important issue for an apparel manufacturer would be the ability to control the selling environment and ensure the adequate ambiance, product display, and customer service.

Interviewer: So what would you recommend to your client?

You: Without knowing more about the company, I might suggest exploring the option of creating a hybrid distribution in which the manufacturer uses both direct and indirect channels. Using indirect channels will allow the manufacturer to achieve rapid distribution and instantly reach many of its target customers. On the other hand, opening its own flagship stores will allow the manufacturer to establish its brand and differentiate it from competitors by offering the right ambiance, product display, and service.

Interviewer: Could you give me an example of a company using a similar distribution model?

You: Well, Nike, Apple, and Sony are using a similar combination of direct and indirect channels, which ensures wide distribution while at the same time enhancing the company's brand image.

Interviewer: Sounds good. Thank you.

CASE COMMENTS: This case explores some of the key issues in setting up a distribution network. The interviewee addresses the case by discussing pros and cons of the three basic distribution models: direct distribution, indirect distribution, and hybrid distribution.

Action-Planning Practice Cases

- Our client is a medium-sized company that makes tires. It wants your help in developing a general competitive strategy and methods to increase profits. How would you advise the client?

- How would you develop a pricing strategy for a luxury hotel chain?

- A computer paper producer is contemplating adding capacity. How should it go about doing this?

- Your client is the owner of a small town amusement park. The local government has offered the client 200 acres of land adjacent to the current amusement park for $15 million dollars. You have been hired to help determine if the client should purchase the land and, if so, what should be done with it.

- You are the CEO of a large construction company that has just been awarded a five-year contract to manage the cleanup of a landfill. The goal is for the area to be waste free in 30 years. How would you accomplish this?

- Your client is a tire manufacturer whose products are not any different from competitors' tires. In addition, the company has no competitive advantages. How would you advise the client to market these tires?

- You are the CEO of a suntan lotion manufacturer that has recently developed a formula to protect customers all day, as opposed to just a few hours like most brands. How would you price your product?

- You are the CEO of a large HMO that is interested in developing a strategic approach to managing its suppliers. How would you manage the company's suppliers to improve its profitability?

- A small plastic materials company has recently developed a new engine part that increases fuel efficiency in cars by 25%. How should it proceed?

- The only alternative rock station in Cleveland, WNUP, recently changed its format to pop rock after a change in management. Since there are now no alternative rock stations in Cleveland, what are the prospects of starting a new alternative rock station?

- A large U.S. gas retailer is considering entering the retail gas market in China. What issues should it consider before it enters the market?

- A large hotel is in the process of evaluating the benefits of its rewards program. How would you determine the value of this program?

- The Chicago Symphony Orchestra currently relies on government grants, as well as public and private donations, to fund its projects. It would like to increase its ticket revenues so it can be less reliant on these donations. You have been hired to help the CSO accomplish its goals. How would you advise the orchestra?

o A bank that makes loans to large real estate developers has a higher-than-industry-average return. Should it increase its capacity?

o A turnaround specialist has recently purchased a large Canadian lumber company that has not been profitable for more than five years. The specialist has hired you to determine how to make the company into a worthwhile purchase. How would you advise her?

o A major pet food manufacturer is seeking to profitably grow sales by 7% in a highly competitive market. The company has six brands. How should these be managed to achieve the client's goals?

o A company that manufactures animal feed has six plants located in the Midwest. Two of the plants are over twenty-five years old and in serious need of refurbishment. Should the company renovate these plants, or build new ones? What issues are involved in this decision?

o Our client is a major U.S. television network that is trying to decide how much to bid for the rights to broadcast the NFL Super Bowl. What factors should it consider?

o The client is a 200-bed hospital in a large city that has not been historically profitable. Recently, new management reorganized the way the hospital functions, and the client has returned significant profits for the last two years. Now the client is considering adding two wings, including accommodations for 300 beds. How would you advise the client regarding this plan?

o Our client is a medium-sized health care company that wants to expand its operations significantly. In the next five years it wants to grow sales and profits by 75%. What recommendations can you make to help the client accomplish this goal?

o A leading internet service provider in Indonesia is considering entering the Japanese market. It has been able to establish itself in Indonesia by charging the lowest subscription fee, making up for low revenues by cutting customer service. Should this company go ahead with its plan?

o Our client is a market-leading fertilizer company whose design team has developed a new formula that boosts the growth of grass while completely inhibiting the growth of all weeds. The company has several other products, each of which targets a single kind of weed, and is concerned that by bringing the new formula to market, it will cannibalize its other products, which are very profitable. How would you advise the client?

o A biotech company has just developed a chemical that helps farmers produce twice as much corn a year. The chemical cost $20MM to develop and is expensive to produce. Should the company attempt to commercialize this product and, if so, how should it be priced?

o A petroleum company has developed a new environmentally friendly gasoline in response to popular new hybrid cars. How can it bring its product to market to maximize the benefit to the company?

Chapter Six

Solving Performance-Gap Cases

Overview

Performance-gap cases depict a company faced with a discrepancy between the desired and the actual state of affairs, between the goal and the reality. To illustrate, a decline in an offering's market share can be viewed as a performance gap between the company's desire to strengthen its market position (goal) and the decrease in market share (reality). Other examples of performance gaps include discrepancies between desired and actual net income, profit margins, and revenues. Typical examples of performance-gap cases are given below.

- *A computer manufacturer is experiencing declining sales. Its product is superior in lifetime and quality to its competitors' products. What would you do?*

- *A shoe manufacturer is gaining market share but has experienced declining profits. What would you do?*

- *You are a product manager for product X. For the past few years your company's market share has been decreasing, even though the overall category was flat. What would you do?*

- *You are the brand manager of a product whose sales have been flat for the last five years. However, the brand's market share has been growing by 5% per year. What's happening with this particular product and what would you do about it?*

- *A company's market share is decreasing and the two options on the table are to lower the price or to advertise. What would you do?*

- *You are the CEO of a large software company. You notice that one of your software products is losing money. What would you do?*

- *Your client, the leading soft drink manufacturer in Brazil, is losing share to one of its competitors. How would you advise your client?*

- *Your client is losing money because of the large number of incoming customer calls. What would you advise?*

- *You are the director of the San Francisco Opera. Ticket sales are down. What would you do?*

- *Your client, a major retail broker, is faced with a declining customer base. How would you address this problem?*

- *Your client, a major satellite radio company, has a problem attracting new customers. What would you advise?*

- *Your client would like to increase its profit margins by 6%. What would be your advice?*

- *Your sales revenues have been declining over the past year. How would you address that?*

- *Your client, McDonald's, is concerned that its growth has been slower than expected. How would you advise the company?*

- *Your client, Eastman Kodak Company, is facing declining sales of its traditional film products due to the growth of digital photography. What would you advise?*

- *Your market share has been declining for the past year. What would you do?*

- *Your client, a large computer game manufacturer, has a difficult time convincing software programmers to develop games for its platform. How would you address this problem?*

Solving Performance-Gap Cases

A relatively simple approach for solving performance-gap problems involves the following three steps: (1) define the problem, (2) identify its primary actionable cause, and (3) develop an action that eliminates the cause, thus solving the problem. These three steps are often referred to as the Problem-Cause-Action (P-C-A) framework (Figure 1) and are discussed in more detail in the following sections.

Figure 1. The P-C-A Framework

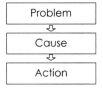

Define the Problem

The performance gap underlying the problem reflects a discrepancy between the company's desired performance, captured in its goal, and its actual performance, indicated by the control metrics. Thus, performance gaps reflect a discrepancy between a desired and an actual performance characteristic such as net income, profit margins, revenues, and market share. This stage of analysis calls for validating the performance gap (verifying that the performance gap really exists rather than, for example, resulting from biased performance metrics), identifying its specifics (e.g., magnitude of the identified discrepancy), and evaluating its overall importance to the company.

Identify the Cause

The key to closing a performance gap is identifying its primary actionable cause. A cause is considered actionable if the company can act on it and devise a solution to remove the cause. To illustrate, the fact that the economy is in a recession is not an actionable cause because the company cannot directly stimulate the economy. Other non-actionable causes include changes in consumer preferences, increasing competition, and various technological, social, legal, and political context factors. On the other hand, factors such as ineffective targeting, inferior product/service, sub-optimal pricing, and inadequate promotion are actionable factors that could be readily removed by the company.

▸ Overview

Because profitability is the ultimate goal for most companies, performance gaps typically are either directly or indirectly related to profitability. Given that profitability is a function of revenues and costs, profitability gaps can be attributed to a decrease in revenues and/or an increase in costs. Here, the decline in revenues can be traced to a decrease in the sales volume and/or a decrease in the per-unit price.[1] The decrease in the sales volume could, in turn, be attributed to one of two factors:

(1) a decline in the unit share of the company's offering relative to competitors or (2) a decline in the unit market size, which affects the sales volume of the company, as well as that of its competitors. Thus, performance gaps can be analyzed in the context of the following profit equation:

$$\text{Profit} = \underbrace{\text{Market share}_{\text{Unit}} \cdot \text{Market size}_{\text{Unit}}}_{\text{Sales volume}} \cdot \text{Price}_{\text{Unit}} - \text{Costs}$$

The above equation also suggests several basic sources for the decline in profitability, as illustrated in Figure 2.

Figure 2. Structuring the Performance Gap

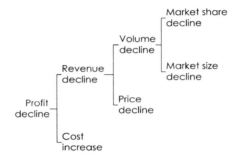

A more detailed analysis of the key strategies for identifying and closing performance gaps is offered in the following sections.

▸ Declining Sales Volume

The decline in sales volume is typically caused by a decrease in the value of the company's offering to its customers relative to that of the competitive offerings. This decline in customer value can be attributed to three main factors: (1) a decline in the attractiveness of the company's offering, (2) an increase in the attractiveness of the competitive offerings, and/or (3) a change in customer needs and preferences. These three factors are discussed in more detail below.

○ *A decline in the value of the company's offering* can be attributed to one or more of the following factors: (1) a decline in the offering's attractiveness from issues such as a reduction in product functionality (e.g., due to a decline in the quality of the raw materials and/or cost-saving technologies), deteriorating service quality (e.g., as a result of outsourcing), weakening brand power (e.g., due to brand dilution from downscale extensions), an increase in price (e.g., as a result of the company's desire to increase margins); (2) a decline in the effectiveness of the company's communications (e.g., due to a decrease in advertising expenditures or ineffective use of communication resources), and/or (3) a decline in the offering's availability to its target customers (e.g., due to low retailer support, frequent stock-outs).

○ *An increase in the value of competitors' offerings* can be attributed to: (1) increased attractiveness of a competitors' offering stemming from factors such as an increase in product functionality, increased service quality, increased brand power, a price cut, or the introduction of new incentives and/or an increase in spending on the current incentives; (2) an increase in the effectiveness of a competitors' communications regarding the offering, and/or (3) an increase in the availability of a competitors' offering to its target customers (e.g., due to increased retailer support). A company's sales volume can also decline due to the introduction of a new offering by its current competitors, as well as by the entry of a new competitor looking to fill the same need of the same target customers.

o *Changes in customer needs and preferences* can decrease the value consumers receive from the offering. For example, consumers can develop a preference for a low-fat and/or low-carbohydrate food which, in turn, will decrease the demand for high-fat and/or high-carbohydrate food. In the same vein, an increase in consumers' price-sensitivity (e.g., in times of an economic downturn) is likely to decrease the demand for higher priced and/or discretionary items.

Note that changes in the value of the company's offering vis-à-vis the value of the competitive offerings is likely to result in a decline in the offering's market share without necessarily affecting the overall market demand (especially when the company has a relatively small market share and/or an undifferentiated product). In contrast, a change in customer preferences is likely to affect the overall market size without necessarily influencing the company's market share (especially in cases when the change applies uniformly to all competitors in the marketplace, e.g., social trends, the state of the economy, government regulations).

▸ Increasing Costs

One approach to analyzing the reasons for an increase in costs is to divide all expenses into three broad categories: cost of goods sold (COGS), marketing costs, and other costs, such as research and development costs, cost of capital, and general and administrative costs.

$$\text{Costs} = \text{Costs of goods sold} + \text{Marketing costs} + \text{Other costs}$$

The drivers of each of these three types of costs are summarized in Figure 3 and discussed in more detail below.

Increase in the Costs of Goods Sold

There are two main causes of an increase in COGS. The first one is an increase in the costs of *inputs*, which involve factors such as the raw materials, labor, and inbound logistics used in developing the company's offering. An increase in the costs of inputs can be addressed by outsourcing, switching suppliers, and adopting alternative technologies that use more cost-effective inputs.

The second factor contributing to an increase in COGS is an increase in the cost of the *processes* that transform the inputs into the end product. An increase in process costs can be addressed by optimizing operations and adopting alternative technologies that use more cost-effective processes.

Figure 3. Cost Analysis Overview

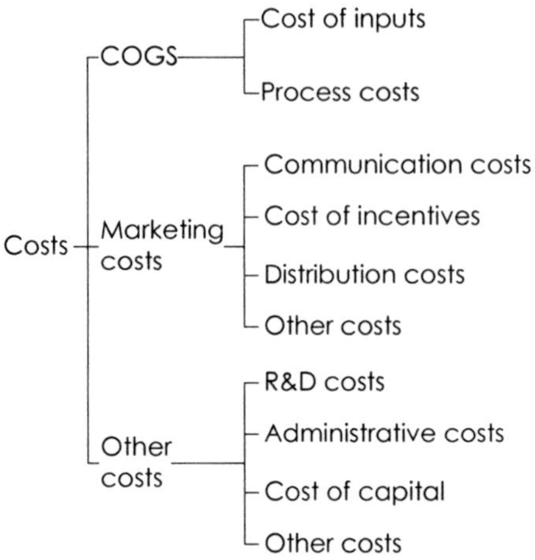

Increase in Marketing Costs

The causes for an increase in marketing costs can be grouped into four categories: communication costs, costs of incentives, distribution costs, and other marketing costs. Each of these four types of expenses is discussed in more detail below.

o   An increase in *communications costs* is typically caused by an increase in advertising expenditures, such as television, radio, print, outdoor, point-of-purchase, and event advertising. Most advertising expenditures are fixed costs; they do not depend on the number of units sold. Note, however, that even though their absolute size remains unchanged regardless of the output volume, advertising costs become progressively smaller per unit of output as volume increases (because the fixed costs are allocated over a larger number of output units).

o   An increase in the *cost of (consumer) incentives* is typically caused by the increased number and/or size of consumer-focused promotions such as price reductions, coupons, rebates, contests, sweepstakes, and premiums. Most incentives (e.g., price reductions, coupons, rebates, premiums) involve variable costs and, unlike mass-media communications, increasing sales volume will not diminish the per-unit cost of the incentives.

o   An increase in *distribution costs* is typically caused by an increase in the margins received by distributors, increased costs of the sales force, and an increase in trade incentives such as trade allowances, volume discounts, and co-op advertising allowances.

o   An increase in *other marketing costs* typically can be attributed to an increase in the costs of factors such as marketing research and marketing overhead.

Increase in Costs Other than COGS and Marketing

In addition to COGS and marketing, an increase in costs can be attributed to other factors such as research and development (R&D), various administrative costs, cost of capital, and other miscellaneous costs.

▸ Declining Margins

In addition to evaluating performance gaps as a function of revenues and costs, performance gaps can be analyzed in terms of unit margins. In this context, unit margins reflect the relationship between an offering's price and its variable costs. Unit margins can be expressed in monetary terms (as the difference in an offering's unit price and its unit variable costs) or as a percentage (as the difference in an offering's unit price and its unit variable costs, which is then divided by the offering's unit price).

Note that calculating margins requires classifying costs into two basic categories: variable and fixed. Fixed costs are expenses that do not fluctuate with output volume within a relevant time period. Typical examples of fixed costs include research and development expenses, mass-media advertising expenses, rent, interest on debt, insurance, plant and equipment expenses, and salary of permanent full-time workers. In contrast, variable costs are expenses that fluctuate in direct proportion to the output volume of units produced. To illustrate, the cost of raw materials and expenses incurred by consumer incentives (e.g., coupons, price discounts, and rebates) are commonly viewed as variable costs. Other expenses such as channel incentives (e.g., promotional allowances) and sales force compensation can be classified either as fixed or variable costs depending on their structure (e.g., fixed salary vs. performance-based compensation). In this context, profitability can be represented as a function of margins as follows:

$$\text{Profit} = \text{Volume} \cdot \underbrace{(\text{Price}_{\text{Unit}} - \text{Variable cost}_{\text{Unit}})}_{\text{Margin}_{\text{Unit}} \, (\$)} - \text{Fixed costs}$$

The above equation also suggests several basic sources for the decline in profitability, as illustrated in Figure 4.

Figure 4. Structuring the Performance Gap as a Function of an Offering's Margins

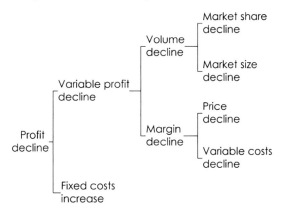

In general, there are two main reasons for declining margins: decline in prices and increase in the variable costs. Decline in prices is typically driven by a company's desire to increase sales volume. Increase in variable costs, on the other hand, is a function of factors such as an increase in the costs of the raw materials, variable labor and distribution costs, and variable promotion costs (e.g., coupons, rebates, discounts, and premiums).

Develop an Action Plan

Once the primary actionable cause has been identified, the next step is to develop a solution that removes the cause and puts the company back on track toward achieving its goal. The key principle in identifying a solution is that it should directly follow from the already identified primary actionable cause of the problem. To illustrate, if a decline in the sales volume has been determined to stem from deteriorating product quality resulting from inferior raw materials, then the logical solution is to improve product quality by identifying alternative sources of raw materials (e.g., replacing suppliers and/or outsourcing).

Note

[1] When assessing the impact of price on revenues and profitability, note that raising the price does not always increase profitability. In product categories where demand is elastic, a price increase might lead to a sizable decline in sales, such that the loss of revenues from the decline in sales volume could be greater than the revenue gain from the price increase.

Performance-Gap Case Examples

Declining Profits (Restaurant Case A)

Interviewer: Your client is a national restaurant chain that has been successful for several years but is now facing decreasing profits. What changes would you recommend to turn its business around?

You: Well, falling profits can be caused by an increase in costs or a decrease in revenues. Has the restaurant faced any increases in costs recently?

Interviewer: No, their costs have remained fairly stable.

You: Then the decreasing profits are most likely a result of decreasing revenues. Now, a decrease in revenues can occur from either a decrease in price or a decrease in volume, so has there been a noticeable decline in the average dining-in check?

Interviewer: No, the average check has remained consistent during the period of declining profit.

You: Since prices do not appear to be the problem, let's look at reasons why the volume of customers might be decreasing. First, we'll examine the potential external factors. Do we know if there has been an increase in competition for the customers that the client targets?

Interviewer: The competition has had the same major players for the last several years, and their market shares have remained fairly consistent.

You: Has there been a change in customer preferences – for instance, by a popular new diet?

Interviewer: No, and the restaurant has a special low-calorie and low-carbohydrate menu selection to appeal to health-conscious customers.

You: Well, so far it does not seem that the decline in profits is caused by external factors. Let's examine some of the key potential internal causes for profit decline. Has there been a change in the advertising strategy of the restaurant?

Interviewer: No. The restaurant has not changed its advertising strategy, and its latest campaign has created a favorable impression with customers.

You: Has the restaurant made any changes in its advertising budget?

Interviewer: Not recently. The restaurant has maintained an advertising budget similar to those of its competitors.

You: Have there been any issues with the wait staff?

Interviewer: There have been complaints by customers about the quality of service, as well the consistency of the food quality.

You: Does the restaurant employ mainly full-time or part-time employees?

Interviewer: The restaurant primarily hires part-time employees.

You: And what is the rationale for this decision?

Interviewer: Part-time employees are hired in order to cut costs.

You: Do you know what the restaurant's policy is for training its staff?

Interviewer: The restaurant currently utilizes on-the-job training instead of a special employee training program.

You: Do we have information about the employee turnover?

Interviewer: The staff tends to be college students who typically work during the summer or else stay with the restaurant for a few years before graduating or moving on to other things.

You: What kind of wages do the part-time employees get?

Interviewer: Typically a little above the minimum wage plus tips.

You: Well, in this case, it seems as though a source of diminishing profits is the decrease in customer volume, which is in part caused by poor quality of service.

Interviewer: So what would you suggest?

You: Well, a good way to develop a better staff is to put a training program in place that acquaints employees with the menu and atmosphere and improves the employees' ability to communicate the restaurant's value to customers. Also, the restaurant could offer better compensation, and eventually increase the percentage of full-time staff.

Interviewer: Good. Now let's move on. Do you have any questions for us regarding the company?

CASE COMMENTS: This is a common case of a company with declining profits. The interviewee identifies the decline in revenues as the primary cause of profit loss and then traces it to a decline in service quality caused by an untrained staff. Another version of the same case, but with a different solution, is offered in the following example.

Declining Profits (Restaurant Case B)

Interviewer: Your client is a national restaurant chain that has been successful for several years but is now facing decreasing profits. What changes would you recommend to turn its business around?

You: Well, falling profits can be caused by an increase in costs or a decrease in revenues. Has the restaurant faced any increases in costs recently?

Interviewer: No, their costs have remained at a fairly stable level.

You: Then the decreasing profits are probably resulting from decreasing revenues. Now, a decrease in revenues can occur from either a decrease in price or a decrease in volume. Has the volume of customers been decreasing?

Interviewer: No. Customer attendance has been stable at almost all restaurant locations.

You: All right. Since volume isn't the problem, let's look at reasons why the price is decreasing. First, has the restaurant recently changed the prices of its menu?

Interviewer: Not recently.

You: Has there been a noticeable decline in the average dining-in check?

Interviewer: Yes, there has been a decline in money spent per customer.

You: Okay. Customers may be spending less based on factors internal or external to the company. In terms of external factors, has there been a recent economic recession that has impacted customer preference?

Interviewer: No, the strength of the economy has not impacted the restaurant's recent performance.

You: Have customers been ordering less because of a new popular diet?

Interviewer: No, and the restaurant has a special low-calorie section with entrée salads.

You: Well, let's look at some other factors within the restaurant. Are portion sizes adequate given the price?

Interviewer: The portions are on par with those offered by the restaurant's major competitors at the same price tier.

You: So, let's break down the meal and make sure that customers are taking advantage of all the restaurant has to offer. For instance, do we know if customers have been staying for dessert?

Interviewer: Actually, dessert sales have been decreasing.

You: Well, since desserts add to the average check per customer a decrease in dessert sales accounts for at least a portion of the declining profits. Has the restaurant recently reduced its dessert menu?

Interviewer: No, the client offers a rotating selection of desserts during the year but always maintains the same assortment size.

You: Then to increase profitability, the restaurant needs to promote its desserts more effectively. Increasing dessert sales would mean higher average dining-in checks, and thus higher revenues and profits. For example, the restaurant might consider featuring dessert advertisements on the dinner tables, as well as encouraging the wait staff to highlight feature desserts to customers. Yet another option is to have a dessert tray so that the customers can see the actual desserts.

Interviewer: Good. Unless there's anything else, I'd like to thank you for coming in today.

CASE COMMENTS: This is a common case of a company with declining profits. The interviewee identifies the decline in revenues as the primary cause of profit loss and then traces it to a decline in the size of the average customer check, caused by a decline in dessert consumption. Another version of the same case, but with a different solution, is offered in the following example.

Declining Profits (Restaurant Case C)

Interviewer: Your client is a national restaurant chain that has been successful for several years but is now facing decreasing profits. What changes would you recommend to turn its business around?

You: Well, falling profits can be caused by an increase in costs or a decrease in revenues. Has the restaurant faced any increases in costs recently?

Interviewer: Actually, there has been an increase in the overall costs of the restaurant.

You: Has there also been a decline in revenues?

Interviewer: No, revenues have remained stable and have been steadily increasing for the last several years.

You: In this case the decline in profitability is apparently caused by an increase in costs. So, let's consider some common scenarios in which a restaurant may be facing increasing costs. Do you know if the restaurant has been facing increasing overhead costs?

Interviewer: No more than their competitors.

You: Do we know if there have been any changes in the cost of labor?

Interviewer: The restaurant has not had any recent increases in wages.

You: What about increasing food costs?

Interviewer: The restaurant actually has been faced with a recent increase in costs associated with ordering and storing food ingredients.

You: Do you know what the restaurant's policy is in choosing its suppliers?

Interviewer: The restaurant purchases its food from several suppliers, and management determines preference of supplier based on price.

You: It could be that this is a logistical problem. Has the staff cited problems of improper purchasing and receiving of food?

Interviewer: The restaurant has contracted with the same trucking agency for several years, and handlers typically do not have many complaints about the stocking system the restaurant has set up.

You: Do we know if there has been a noticeable increase in waste and leftovers during food preparation?

Interviewer: The cooking staff has been instructed to pay close attention to reducing waste, so leftover cuts of meat are not typically a problem.

You: Have the increases in ingredients and storage resulted directly from an increased demand for food by the restaurant, perhaps because of a recent change in the menu?

Interviewer: The restaurant's menu recently has been extensively expanded to provide customers with a wider array of choice.

You: So how many entrees does the restaurant typically offer to customers?

Interviewer: About 20.

You: And how many entrees are typical for a comparable restaurant?

Interviewer: About 12.

You: Is the extra variety of entrees an integral part of the restaurant's positioning strategy?

Interviewer: No.

You: Do we know why the restaurant offers an assortment of entrees that is almost twice as large as that of its competitors?

Interviewer: It's an experimental program implemented by the new management.

You: Well, since revenues have remained fairly stable for the last several years it doesn't seem as though the menu expansion has contributed to any noticeable gains. Furthermore, the costs associated with the expanded menu, such as purchasing and storing ingredients, have actually been hurting the restaurant's profitability. Thus, to increase profitability, the restaurant might consider cutting down its menu selection and in the future conducting a more careful cost-benefit analysis before making any major changes.

Interviewer: Good. It was nice meeting you. We'll keep in touch.

CASE COMMENTS: This is a common case of a company with declining profits. The interviewee identifies the increase in costs as the primary cause of profit loss and then traces it to an increase in the entrée assortment.

Declining Profits (Cookie Manufacturer Case)

Interviewer: Our client is a cookie manufacturer that is a market leader and has recently been experiencing decreasing profits. To reverse this trend, they are considering launching a new advertising campaign. Is this a good idea?

You: Well, falling profits can be caused by an increase in costs or a decrease in revenues. Has the company faced any recent cost increases?

Interviewer: Actually the company's costs have been decreasing for several years.

You: That's interesting. Since both profits and costs are going down, I think it's safe to say that the company's sales are down significantly. Is this correct?

Interviewer: Yes. The company's sales began slipping two years ago, and have now declined sharply.

You: A decrease in sales revenues can be caused by a decrease in volume or a decrease in price. Has the client lowered its prices recently?

Interviewer: The company has been lowering prices on its cookie products over the last few years.

You: Do we know if the client's competition has also been cutting its prices?

Interviewer: No, their prices have been relatively steady. The company used to maintain a premium price over its competitors but has reduced its price for several years; it stopped only recently, when the price was roughly equal to the competition, and it has remained there since.

You: Well, lowering prices is certainly one factor that might account for the decrease in sales revenues. Another potential factor is the sales volume. Do we have information on changes in the volume of cookies that customers have been purchasing?

Interviewer: The company's sales volume has been decreasing for about two years.

You: That is somewhat unusual. One would expect that lowering prices should result in an increase, not a decrease, in sales volume. So, we need to examine the reasons why, despite a decrease in price relative to its competition, our client's sales volume is still decreasing.

Interviewer: Go ahead.

You: One possibility is that the decline in sales volume is caused by disruptions in the product's availability. Have there been changes in the way the client's suppliers or distributors operate that are hindering the stocking of cookie products at supermarket locations?

Interviewer: Our client has been using the same distributors for years, and there have not been any problems in terms of a shortage of supply.

You: Another possibility is that the decline in sales volume is a function of a change in customer preferences. Do we know if there has been a significant change in preferences recently that may have caused such a substantial drop in volume of sales?

Interviewer: Well, it's difficult to answer a question about consumer preference with certainty.

You: I understand. Have competitors who manufacture similar products also been suffering from lagging sales in recent years?

Interviewer: No, actually the client's competition has been doing well.

You: This rules out a change in customer preferences. Has there been an increase in competition in the client's market?

Interviewer: No, the market has had the same major players for several years.

You: Do we know if a competitor has been gaining a significant share in the market at the expense of our client?

Interviewer: Over the last two years, all of the client's major competitors have been increasing their share of the market while the client's share has been decreasing.

You: The fact that all competitors are gaining share at the client's expense seems to indicate that this is a result of a company-specific weakness. You mentioned earlier that costs have been decreasing in the company. Has the company cut down on its advertising budget?

Interviewer: After profits started dipping a year ago company management reacted by increasing their advertising budget.

You: Well, the decrease in costs has to be coming from somewhere. Has the company done something to tamper with the quality of product in order to cut costs – such as, say, changing the recipe of its cookies?

Interviewer: Yes. A few years ago management decided to reuse cookie crumbs and use less expensive ingredients in order to cut costs.

You: And following from what you said earlier, I'm guessing that the lower quality of product was the way that the client justified lowering its prices.

Interviewer: Most likely.

You: Well, it seems that we can identify why the client's sales volume has been decreasing. It sounds as if, over the last several years, the company has been trying to cut costs, probably in order to maintain or increase profit margins. Because of the inferior product quality, however, the sales volume started to decline rather than increase.

To reverse the decline in the sales volume, the company started to lower its prices. Nevertheless, as more and more customers started realizing that the product quality had deteriorated, they began switching to competitors' products. Apparently, the company's customers were not very price sensitive, and for them product quality was of primary importance. This is consistent with the fact that a few years back they were the market leader despite higher prices.

Interviewer: So would you recommend that the client increase its advertising expenditures?

You: Well, this is definitely a problem that an increase in advertising by itself would not be able to solve. In fact, if the company increases its advertising without improving the product, it will essentially be encouraging more customers to buy its inferior products.

Interviewer: So what do you suggest the client should do?

You: The first step is to improve the product. It is also important to realize that, at this point, simply restoring the original product is not enough to change the perception of brand quality in the minds of its former customers.

Interviewer: So why not advertise to improve brand image?

You: Advertising is definitely an option worth considering. The company might try to promote the product as "new and improved." The drawback of this approach is that customers might not necessarily be convinced that the quality has been improved to a point consistent with their preferences. So, instead of advertising, I would suggest exploring the option of having customers experience the improved product rather than simply telling them about it.

Interviewer: And how would you propose that the company should do this?

You: One option would be to send free trial-size samples to customers in its key target markets. Another option is to have product samples in distribution outlets where the product is being sold. Once customers experience the improved taste of the company's cookies they would be more likely to consider switching back.

Interviewer: Great. Let's move on to something else. Do you have any questions about our company?

CASE COMMENTS: The case depicts a common scenario of declining corporate profits. The interviewee identifies that the profit decline was most likely a result of deterioration of the quality of the company's product, which in turn was caused by the implementation of cost-cutting measures such as using inferior product ingredients. To address the problem, the interviewee proposes improving product quality and launching a promotional campaign focused on product trials to let customers experience the improved product.

Declining Sales Revenues (Odor Freshener Case)

Interviewer: Our client has created a new kind of household odor freshener. After reaching its sales goals the first year, sales in its second year on the market are lower than anticipated. What suggestions would you make to the client in order to improve its performance?

You: Can you tell me more about the product?

Interviewer: Well, the product is an active odor neutralizer. It's designed to be sprayed directly onto the source of bad odors, which it replaces with a fresh scent.

You: What's new about it?

Interviewer: It's a hybrid between a stationary air freshener such as a plug-in, and stronger cleaners and sanitizers.

You: Does the product actually have any cleaning properties, or is it exclusively an odor reducer?

Interviewer: The product, used by itself, would not properly clean a spill or clean out a trash can. It is meant exclusively to neutralize bad odors at their source.

You: Since the product's initial year was successful, we need to find out what happened in the second year. Do we know if new competitors entered the market for odor fresheners?

Interviewer: There were no new competitors.

You: Were there any changes in the product formula?

Interviewer: No changes were made to the formulation.

You: Were there any changes to the product's price?

Interviewer: The price remained unchanged.

You: When launching the product, did we offer any incentives such as coupons?

Interviewer: Yes.

You: Are we still offering these incentives?

Interviewer: Yes.

You: Did we change anything in the distribution channel?

Interviewer: No, the product is available at the same retailers.

You: No changes in the amount of shelf space, location within the store, availability?

Interviewer: No.

You: Did we make any changes to the advertising campaign?

Interviewer: The advertising expenditures were, of course, larger the first year, which is typical for a new product launch. After reaching a substantial penetration rate, the advertising was trimmed down to a minimal amount – similar to what the company has done with its other products.

You: Was there a drop in sales for those other products?

Interviewer: There was a small decline, of course, but not nearly of the magnitude of this product.

You: So, it seems that we did not make any changes to our marketing plan and, nevertheless, sales were declining.

Interviewer: Yes.

You: Well, the decline in sales can be caused by one of two factors: either fewer customers are using the product – which indicates a problem with the product – or the cause is the frequency with which the customers use the product rather than the number of customers per se. Do we know if customers that purchase the product are happy with it, and want to buy it again?

Interviewer: Research surveys indicate that customers are satisfied with the product and the repurchase rate is high.

You: So, it does not seem that the decline in sales is caused by a decline in product usage. Do we have any information on how often customers are using the product?

Interviewer: We don't really know, but a recent consumer focus group indicated that customers on average use the product about once a week.

You: Does the client know how often customers ideally should use the product?

Interviewer: Well, to receive the maximum benefits, the odor freshener should be used every day.

You: In this case, the low number of usage occasions is one issue that the client can address in order to bring up its revenue.

Interviewer: Are there any other issues?

You: Yes, in addition to the frequency of usage, the overall consumption also depends on the quantity used on each occasion.

Interviewer: How is usage frequency different from usage quantity?

You: Well, usage frequency indicates how many times a product is used in a given timeframe, say weekly; usage quantity refers to the amount that customers use on each occasion.

Interviewer: So, what would you recommend to the client?

You: I would suggest a two-prong solution that involves increasing usage frequency and usage quantity.

Interviewer: Tell me more about the two.

You: Usage frequency can be increased by a promotional campaign explicitly designed to create top-of-mind awareness of how often the product should be used. The goal is to create a habit, so that the use of this product becomes a regular part of consumers' daily lives.

Increasing usage quantity can also be achieved by educating customers about different ways that the odor freshener can be used. For instance, Arm & Hammer encourages customers to use their baking soda for baking, cleaning, brushing their teeth, exfoliating their skin, and so on. So the company should highlight common situations in a household when the product can be used – such as freshening a frequently used couch or rug, eliminating odor caused by a pet, freshening a car, or reducing the odor from a smelly garbage bag.

Interviewer: What about usage quantity?

You: Usage quantity can be increased by focusing customers' attention on the amount sprayed each time they use the product. This can be achieved by an advertising campaign that goes beyond creating product awareness among target customers to teach them how often the product should be used. We could also communicate this through packaging. For example, we could add instructions that say "Spray twice for extra freshness" or "Spray until surface is damp."

Interviewer: If you had to summarize your solution in one short sentence, what would it be?

You: Focus company efforts on having customers use more of their product more frequently. This should take care of sales revenues.

Interviewer: Good. I'm sure we'll be in touch. Thanks for coming in today.

CASE COMMENTS: This case involves a company with declining sales revenues of a new product after a successful launch. The interviewee evaluates the potential sources of this decline, such as increased competition and changes in the company's marketing strategy and tactics (e.g., changes in the product formulation, pricing, incentives, communication, and distribution). The solution, however, appears to be in the way customers use the product and, in particular, the frequency of usage and quantity used per occasion.

Increase in Costs (Mail-Order Company)

Interviewer: Your client is a mail-order flower company that has been experiencing declining profits despite an increase in sales. What is the problem and how would you remedy the situation?

You: What exactly is it that a mail-order flower company does?

Interviewer: Well, it mails catalogs to potential customers, who then order flowers by phone or internet to place an order.

You: Okay, let me think about this for a second. In general, declining profits can either be caused by decreasing revenues or increasing costs. Since we know that revenues are actually up, this means that costs have risen even higher. So, let's start by identifying the primary cause of this rise in costs.

Interviewer: How would you do that?

You: In the case of a mail-order flower company I can think of a few reasons for an increase in costs, mainly through an increase in the cost of goods sold or an increase in marketing expenses.

Interviewer: Walk me through these.

You: Sure. With regard to the cost of goods sold, has the company experienced an increase in the cost of purchasing flowers?

Interviewer: No, it has not.

You: Has there been an increase in packaging or delivery expenses?

Interviewer: No. Shipping expenses have remained stable.

You: Are there any other major costs of goods sold that have increased for the client?

Interviewer: None that we know of.

You: Okay, then we can conclude that the increase in cost is not caused by an increase in costs of the goods sold. Another source of increasing costs could be from an increase in marketing expenses. For a mail-order flower company, some common sources for an increase in expenses could be expenses arising from advertising or direct mail such as catalogs. So, to start with, has there been an increase in advertising expenditure, such as TV and radio commercials?

Interviewer: No.

You: Has the company recently increased its expenditure on direct mail, such as catalogs?

Interviewer: Yes. The client has recently increased the number of catalogs it mails out.

You: Well this could be the source of the increase in costs that we are looking for. Was the client profitable before the new catalog campaign?

Interviewer: Yes.

You: I want to know more about the new catalog campaign. Can you tell me how many more catalogs are being sent out now, than before?

Interviewer: Catalog distribution has increased from 3 million to 5 million.

You: I'm assuming that these 2 million new addresses are new customers that had not previously purchased from the client, is this correct?

Interviewer: Yes.

You: Do we know how the company acquired the 2 million new addresses to which it mails catalogs?

Interviewer: Last year the company purchased a database of addresses based on drivers' license information from the DMV. This database provided the addresses of 2 million new households.

You: This new campaign might be a source of the company's problem. Do we know the yield on the 2 million new catalogs?

Interviewer: It is currently around 2%.

You: Okay, so that means for every one hundred customers that receive a catalog, two will make an order. Now let's calculate the contribution that the company receives from these two customers. In order to do that we need to know the gross margin as well as the average order size.

Interviewer: Sure, the gross margin is 50% and the average customer order is $56.

You: This means that the contribution the client receives is (50% · $56), which equals $28. Given a yield of 2% in a set of 100 customers, this would mean revenues to the company of $56.

Interviewer: Okay.

You: Now, let's deal with costs. How much does each catalog cost the company in terms of product costs, and mailing expenses?

Interviewer: Each catalog costs the client $.62 in production costs and $.08 in mailing costs.

You: Okay, so this means a cost of ($.62+$.08) or $.70 per catalog. For a set of 100 catalogs this comes out to a cost of $70.

Interviewer: Good, so what does this mean?

You: Well, this means that the client loses ($56-$70), or about $14 per hundred catalogs. So, it is certainly an increase in costs that is hurting the profitability of the company because the yield on the catalogs is too low to maintain profitability.

Interview: So what do we do?

You: One way to address this issue is to cut the costs of producing the catalogs, so that profitability can be achieved.

Interviewer: All right. Any other solutions?

You: Sure. Another course of action is to improve the targeting of catalog mailings. Do we know who the client currently sends catalogs to?

Interviewer: All consumers between the ages of 20 and 60 from the mailing list.

You: Does the mailing list include both men and women?

Interviewer: Yes. It is about 50-50.

You: And how often do we mail out catalogues?

Interviewer: Six times a year.

You: So we send catalogues at even intervals or around certain dates?

Interviewer: Catalogues are mailed out at even intervals every two months.

You: Okay, so one way to improve the return on catalogues is to improve the scheduling of the catalog mailings, focusing on times of year when people tend to buy flowers, such as Mother's Day, Christmas, and Valentine's Day.

Interviewer: Anything else?

You: In addition, we can also consider having separate mailing schedules for men and women. Unlike women, who are likely to buy flowers year-round to decorate their homes, men are likely to buy flowers primarily around Valentine's Day and Mother's Day. Thus, we could reduce the off-season mailing to men and send them catalogs only for Valentine's Day and Mother's Day.

Interviewer: Good. It was great meeting and talking with you. Good luck and have a great day.

CASE COMMENTS: This is a common case examining a company dealing with a decline in profits despite an increase in revenues. By eliminating potential sources one by one, the interviewee identifies the increase in costs as the primary cause for the decline in profits and offers a solution to reduce the costs.

Adding Manufacturing Capacity (Snack-Bar Case)

Interviewer: Our client has recently introduced a new snack bar to the market. Sales in the first month have surpassed the client's projections, and the client is considering adding capacity. What advice would you give?

You: Does the client have any insight into what might have caused the high demand for their products?

Interviewer: No. The client is not sure.

You: Let's start by identifying the cause of the strong demand by looking at the product. What's unique about this snack bar that sets it apart?

Interviewer: The snack bar is organic, with no preservatives or artificial flavors. It's high in vitamins and minerals, and promoted as containing no trans fats, high fructose corn syrup, or hydrogenated oils.

You: Well, it seems like the product is appealing to health-conscious customers. How does the client promote the snack bar?

Interviewer: The client utilizes mass-media channels, hoping to get the word out about its snack bar to as many people as possible. To do this, they focus their advertising efforts on sports and health magazines and newspapers.

You: Okay. And how is the product priced?

Interviewer: The snack bar is priced at a premium relative to its competitors because of its organic content.

You: Do we know if the company provided any incentives, such as coupons or volume discounts, in the first weeks of its product launch that might have caused these greater than expected sales?

Interviewer: There were no major incentives.

You: Do we know if the client's distribution is limited to supermarkets, or does it includes other outlets — for instance, nutrition stores.

Interviewer: In addition to major supermarkets and grocery stores, the product is available in public locations such as offices, fitness facilities, and schools across the country.

You: Do we know if the sales have been evenly distributed across geographic areas. Have there been greater sales in, say, urban areas?

Interviewer: The sales have been somewhat sporadic nationwide, with the exception of California, where sales have been significantly higher than elsewhere.

You: Would it be fair to say that most of the excess demand comes from California?

Interviewer: Yes.

You: Then the question is: What is different about California? In general, California residents are likely to be more health-conscious and, therefore, prefer the organic snack-bar. But then, this is not the only organic snack on the market. So, it could be something else. Do we know if someone endorsed the snack-bar, for example, as a part of a diet or a nutrition plan?

Interviewer: The client is unaware of anyone endorsing this snack. However, the California state legislature recently passed a new bill limiting the fat and sugar content in food that is offered within the state's school system, and the client's snack bar qualifies for distribution in California schools.

You: Are there any competitor snack bars that also qualify for distribution in California schools?

Interviewer: At this time, there are only a few.

You: Would it be fair to say that the demand from California schools accounts for the greater sales in California?

Interviewer: More or less.

You: In this case, we can conclude that the excess demand for the snack is driven by its adoption by the California school system. In order to decide whether to invest in additional capacity, the client needs to evaluate the sustainability of its market position as one of the only snacks qualified for distribution in California schools.

Interviewer: Do you think this advantage is sustainable?

You: If the market is profitable – and most likely it is – soon most of the players in the snack bar market will develop similar offerings. As a result, our client's bar will likely loose its position as the only bar that fits the new bill. In this context, the client should focus on building on its pioneering advantage to differentiate its brand and clearly position its product in the minds of its customers. Without a sustainable competitive advantage, the demand for the snack bar is likely to fall soon after new competitors enter the market. In this context, expanding capacity without differentiating the product might lead to future overcapacity.

Interviewer: Great. We'll give you a call later this week.

CASE COMMENTS: The case posits a reverse performance-gap problem: the demand for a company's products exceeds its initial projections, leading it to consider investing in extra manufacturing capacity. Following a series of probing questions, the interviewee identifies the source of the extra demand – a recently passed state bill which de facto made the company's snack bar one of the few qualifying for distribution in the California school system. In this context, the decision to invest in extra capacity hinges on the company's ability to sustain its pioneering advantage in this market.

Performance-Gap Practice Cases

- A car manufacturer was gaining market share but experienced declining profits. You have been hired to help address the situation. What recommendations would you make?

- Your client is a manufacturer of CDs. You have been hired to find out why there has been an alarming decline in profitability. How would you find the source of this problem, and what suggestions would you make?

- Your client is a mall-based jewelry store that has recently faced declining profits. How would you advise the client?

- A cable company with access to over 10 million customers in Illinois has failed to return a profit in the past two years. You have been hired to help the company determine what it is doing wrong. How would you advise it?

- You have been approached by an agricultural equipment business whose major product line, tractors, is losing money. What recommendations can you make to the client to help turn its business around?

- Your client is a newspaper that has been experiencing declining readership and, thus, declining profitability. How would you advise the client?

- Your client is a soap manufacturer that has been in the business for almost 100 years. Despite years of steady business and profits, the last three quarters have been below expectations. What recommendations can you make?

- You have been called in by a major accounting firm that has experienced declining profits in its auditing operations. What recommendations would you make to help the firm improve profitability?

- A regional trucking company has been losing money for the last several years. Other trucking companies have also been experiencing a loss in profits. Why is this happening, and what suggestions can you make to fix this problem?

- A major home insurance company is experiencing low growth. Its more price-focused competitors have been stealing market share. Management believes that this problem can be solved through increasing product differentiation. What suggestions can you make to address low growth?

- Your company is a candy producer that originally started as a single product company but has recently expanded its product line. Management is concerned because while sales have grown since the product line expansion, profitability has not. How would you handle this situation?

- Our client is a chemical manufacturer who produces a food preservative used mainly for frozen dinners. Despite an increase in market share, the company is experiencing declining profits. How would you advise our client?

- You have been hired by an online computer store to help address numerous complaints about poor customer relations. What suggestions would you make?

o   A major U.S. beer company entered the Australian market three years ago. However, despite a large market, sales have been very disappointing. You have been hired to address the situation. How would you advise your client?

o   A drug manufacturer in the southwestern U.S. has requested your assistance in addressing high costs. It feels that its overhead is much higher than that of its competitors. As a consultant, how would you help solve this problem?

o   A life insurance company currently has pre-tax profits of $20MM, while the industry average ranges between $30MM and $40.5MM. Why are they making less than the industry?

o   You are the manufacturer of an electrical component for colored cell phone screens, but you have failed to make a profit for the last several years despite a huge increase in demand for such equipment. Why?

o   Eureka, Inc. is an established brand of cosmetic products in Europe. The company's product line is developed from the same set of raw materials and production methods, and the company has worked with the same distributors for several years. Eureka's profits, which were once substantial, have been shrinking for several years. What can this company do to increase its profits?

o   You are the CEO of a consumer finance bank that specializes in high-risk lending. Recently you tried to introduce a new product aimed at individuals with a much higher credit score. This product failed. How would you address this situation?

o   Our client is an established food wholesaler that is experiencing a decline in sales. This confounds the management, since many of the company's competitors are experiencing a large increase in sales. How would you advise the client?

o   A middle-of-the-pack consumer product company has been experiencing diminishing sales for its leading shampoo brand. What recommendations can you make?

o   Your client is a cell phone manufacturer. The company's financial performance has been slipping for the last two years, and the client is most concerned about its falling return on investment. How would you advise the client?

o   A global razor brand launched two new products last year. While sales have gone up 15%, management is concerned about lagging margins. What is the impact on profitability likely to be, and what recommendations can you make?

o   A clothing company has noticed a decline in its women's apparel department. How can it reverse this?

Chapter Seven

Solving External-Change Cases

Overview

External-change cases depict scenarios that involve a change in the environment in which the company operates. To illustrate, external-change cases involve questions such as evaluating the impact of a competitive action (e.g., new product introduction, price change, aggressive incentives and communications, new distribution channels, changes in customer demand, changes in technology, revised legal regulations and government policies). Typical examples of external-change cases are given below.

- *Your competitor just lowered its price. What do you do?*

- *Your competitor just launched an aggressive advertising campaign. What do you do?*

- *What would you do if R&D told you that they had come up with a pasta sauce that lowers cholesterol?*

- *How should Fatburger (fast food chain) react to consumers' obsession with fat-free food?*

- *How should Segway react to state laws restricting the use of Segways on sidewalks?*

- *Your client, a large sports club, is successfully operating in an upscale urban neighborhood. A developer announces plans to build a residential complex nearby that will also include a sports club that will directly compete with your client's club. How would you advise your client?*

- *Your brand has experienced substantial share erosion for the past several years because of a competitor that claims to be "better." Under what circumstances should you reformulate your product?*

- *Your client is a high-end sports car manufacturer that is concerned about vulnerability to market cycles. What is your advice?*

- *What is the impact of rising gasoline prices on McDonald's sales?*

- *Your client makes hydraulic pumps and is concerned about vulnerability to market cycles. What should it do?*

- *Our client is a regional retail bank that has recently faced increased competition from new Internet-based financial services firms. Deposits are decreas-*

ing, and the client is looking to grow its bottom line. As a consultant, how would you advise the client?

o   *For the last 20 years you have been the only major parcel delivery service in Australia. Recently a new firm entered the market, and while it has only stolen 15% of market share, your profits are down by almost 25%. How would you address the situation?*

o   *You are the CEO of an old tire manufacturing plant. How do you regard the threat of a competitor that has built a new facility in the same area?*

o   *Discover has faced strong competition from new credit cards entering the market and is considering dropping its $50 annual fee. Is this a good idea?*

o   *Your client is a large national telephone company that is concerned about losing share to new broadband phone companies. Is this a valid concern? What advice would you have for the client?*

Solving External-Change Cases

This type of case involves evaluating the impact of a significant change in the context in which the company operates. In general, there are four main types of external changes: (1) changes in the customer base (e.g., changes in customer demographics, buying power, needs, and preferences), (2) changes in the competitive environment (e.g., a new competitive entry or a change in the strategy and/or tactics of a competitive offering, such as adding new product features, lowering price, launching an aggressive advertising campaign); (3) changes in collaborator environment; and (4) changes in the social, technological, economic, political, legal, and physical context. Note that these four types of external changes can be related to the four Cs which, combined with the fifth C (company), comprise the 5-C framework. Note also that when the unit of consideration is a particular strategic business unit within the company, changes that take place in the company (e.g., changes in the management, operations, and/or internal resources) can also be viewed as external changes from the viewpoint of this business unit.

Cases involving an external change can be best solved by using the following three-step approach: (1) understand the specifics of the external *change*, (2) evaluate the likely *impact* of the change on the offering's performance, and (3) develop the optimal *action*. These three steps comprise the Change-Impact-Action (C-I-A) framework (Figure 1) and are discussed in more detail below.

Figure 1. The C-I-A Framework

Understand the External Change

Understanding the external change involves two key aspects: identifying the specifics of the change and identifying its key drivers. These two factors are discussed in more detail below.

o Identifying the *specifics* of the external change aims at pinpointing its key aspects, such as content, timing, and magnitude. For example, if the change involves a competitive price reduction, the specifics would involve factors such as the depth and expected duration of the price reduction. If the change involves an aggressive competitive advertising campaign, the specifics would involve factors such as message, frequency, and coverage.

o Identifying the *drivers* of the external change involves establishing its likely cause(s). For example, in addition to being motivated by the desire to "steal" a company's customers, a competitive price cut can be caused by a variety of other factors such as inventory management issues (e.g., reducing the on-hand inventory) and product line management issues (e.g., minimizing cannibalization of a company's other products). Identifying the drivers is extremely important because it enables the company to optimize its response. To illustrate, a competitive price cut driven by inventory clearance is likely to be short-lived and will typically require a different response than a price cut motivated by an aggressive repositioning of the competitor's offering aimed at "stealing" the company's customers.

Evaluate the Impact of the Change on the Company

After the specifics and the drivers of the external change have been identified, the next step is to evaluate their impact on the company's offering. In general, depending on their impact on the company, external changes can be viewed as opportunities, threats, or neutral factors.

o *Opportunities* are factors that are likely to have a favorable impact on the company's offering. Factors typically considered as opportunities involve the introduction of new favorable government regulations, a competitor's exit, or an increase in consumer demand.

o *Threats* are factors that are likely to have an unfavorable impact on the company's offering. Factors typically considered as threats involve a new competitive entry, actions bolstering the attractiveness of a competitor's offerings (e.g., new product introduction, price cut, aggressive incentives and communications), changes in customer demand, changes in technology, legal regulations, and government policies.

o *Neutral factors* are unlikely to have material impact on the company's offering. For example, certain regulatory changes, technological developments, competitive actions, and customer trends might not be directly related to a company's offering and, therefore, can be considered irrelevant from the viewpoint of value analysis.

Note that classifying external changes into one of the above three categories is rather subjective: The same factor can be considered favorable, unfavorable, or neutral, depending on a manager's assumptions about the likely drivers of the external change and their impact on the value proposition of the company's offering.

Develop the Optimal Action in Response to the Change

After evaluating the impact of the external change on the company's offering, the next step is to develop the optimal response and revise the company's business plan accordingly.

The company's response is contingent on its evaluation of the likely impact of the change. Thus, if the change is viewed as an opportunity, then the response will involve augmenting the company's business plan to take advantage of this opportunity. If the change is deemed to be a threat, then the response will involve modifying the company's plan to minimize the potential damage from the threat. Finally, if the change is not likely to have a material impact on the company, then no changes to the company's business plan are required.

External-Change Case Examples

New Competitive Entry (Fork Lift Case)

Interviewer: You are the vice president of an established fork lift manufacturer. A contact from one of your loyal customers has just notified you that you need to lower your price by 5% or another company will win the bid for supplying their new project. What would you do?

You: First, I want to make sure I understand the situation correctly. Can you tell me why our customers are asking us to lower our prices now?

Interviewer: Your customer's purchasing department solicits multiple bids and prioritizes price when making a final decision. Recently, competitors from Taiwan have entered the market and are offering similar products at prices that are lower than our original price by 10%.

You: The obvious solution seems to be to cut the price by 5%. This, however, will lead to a decline in sales revenues and even greater decline in profits on this sale. Moreover, once we offer a lower price to a customer, it would be difficult not to offer similar discounts in the future. We might have to start offering similar discounts on other products and to other customers as well. So, before going ahead with cutting the price, it might be worthwhile to explore alternative options.

Let's start with the customers. Do we know what characteristics are important to customers when buying our products?

Interviewer: Price is definitely important, especially to the purchasing department. Also, in addition to functional characteristics such as power and capacity, other important factors are durability, reliability, warranty, and customer service. These factors are especially important for project managers.

You: Do we know how well we do relative to the competitors in these attributes?

Interviewer: Well, in terms of functionality, our forklift is identical to competitors' forklifts. The real differences in our product are the durability, reliability, warranty, and customer service, on which our product is superior.

You: So what we really need to understand is why the customer is not willing to pay extra for these benefits. Do we have any insight about this?

Interviewer: No. This is your assignment.

You: I see. One possibility is that the purchasing department is mostly concerned about price and might not readily see the true value of the intangible benefits such as durability, reliability, warranty, customer service. Or, they might see the value but not know how much premium to place on this. In fact, this seems to be the case since they are willing to pay more for our product relative to the competitors.

Interviewer: So what would you do?

You: Well, what we need to do in this case is to find a way to express the value of these intangible benefits in monetary terms.

Interviewer: And how would you do that?

You: Let's first monetize durability. We need to find out how much more durable our product is than competitors' products. For example, let's say our product provides two extra years of fork lift usage. We can convert this extra lifetime into monetary terms and find the value that these two extra years of usage offers customers. Do we happen to know this number?

Interviewer: Let's say it's $6,000.

You: Great. So next we have to find out the monetary value of the extra reliability. One way to calculate this is by finding how many fewer breakdowns we have per year than our competitors. Then calculate the downtime cost for the company over the lifetime of the forklift.

Interviewer: Let's assume that our client's products have on average two less breakdowns per year, which over the lifetime of the fork lifts saves the company $5,000.

You: Now we should consider the amount customers save as a result of our superior warranty. First, however, on what basis is our warranty superior?

Interviewer: Essentially, our products come with a longer warranty, which covers service calls and replacement parts.

You: In that case, we need to calculate the total cost for the number of service calls and the value of replacement parts over the extra warranty we offer relative to competitors.

Interviewer: Say, this comes out to $7,000.

You: Okay. Finally, we should consider the dollar value of superior customer service. Do we know what constitutes superior customer service?

Interviewer: The most important factor of customer service is response time, since this results in shorter downtime for the fork lift and the customer's operations.

You: In this case, we need to calculate the total number of calls that a client is likely to make over the lifetime of the forklift, and identify the amount they save as a result of our faster response time.

Interviewer: Assume that's $9,000.

You: Great. What we need to do now is calculate the total dollar value of these benefits. Let's see, the monetary value for the extra durability is $6,000, plus $5,000 the client saves as a result of fewer breakdowns by our more reliable product, plus the $7,000 saved by our customers due to our longer warranty, and finally the $9,000 that customers save as a result of faster customer service. This adds up to $27,000. Now, do we know what the price of the fork lift is?

Interviewer: The original selling price is $220,000.

You: Okay, so let's see. If our price is $220,000, and the competitors' price is 10% less, this means that their fork lifts are priced at $198,000, and our price premium is $22,000. This means that despite the price premium, our fork lifts offer greater value to customers.

Interviewer: So, what would be your recommendation?

You: Instead of lowering the price, I would suggest developing a value-analysis report for the client that delineates the monetary value of our added benefits, demonstrating that in spite of its higher price, our products are actually more cost-efficient. Thus, we can show that even though our forklift is priced $22,000 higher than the competition, it offers extra benefits amounting to $27,000. So essentially, we offer our forklifts at a $5,000 discount.

Interviewer: Good.

CASE COMMENTS: This case presents a scenario in which increasing global competition puts pressure on a local manufacturer's prices. The interviewee proposes that instead of lowering prices and potentially entering into a price war, the company find better ways to communicate its value to the customer. To achieve that, the interviewee calculates the monetary value of the product's intangible benefits and shows that despite its higher price, the company's offering is actually more cost-efficient.

Dealing with an Economic Downturn (Ritz-Carlton Case)

Interviewer: You are the general manager of The Ritz Carlton, Kuala Lumpur. Recently, forest fires close to the city have wrecked the tourism industry, as well as the regional economy. As a result, occupancy in hotels across the area has suffered. Many of your competitors have decided to cut prices in order to draw more customers. What would your response be to these new developments?

You: First, I would like to know more about how severely we have been impacted. Can you tell me what our current occupancy levels are?

Interviewer: The Ritz Carlton, Kuala Lumpur has 250 guest rooms, of which only 37% are currently occupied.

You: And how does this fare relative to expected occupancy levels at this time during the year?

Interviewer: About 75% of rooms are typically occupied this time of year.

You: Is this situation similar to what competitors were facing before they cut their prices?

Interviewer: Yes, but after lowering their prices, our competitors in the luxury hotel market have improved their occupancy levels to about 50%.

You: Well, an action that we can explore is cutting prices as the competition has done. It is definitely one way to draw more customers. However, lowering prices has some significant drawbacks.

Interviewer: Like what?

You: Given the current image of The Ritz Carlton worldwide, lowering prices at one of our locations will harm our brand equity. Moreover, we are likely to attract a different demographic if we lower prices – like younger families with more children, for instance. This risks alienating our core customer base. Thus, while boosting sales in the short run, cutting prices will cost us in the long run.

Interviewer: How else would you address this issue if not by lowering price?

You: Well, rather than cutting the price of staying at our hotel, we could improve the benefits we offer to our guests.

Interviewer: How would you do that?

You: We could offer upgrades to better rooms, and add extra services such as limousine service to greet our guests at the airport. This way we can maintain our brand image while giving customers an incentive to choose our hotel.

Interviewer: Why do you think this strategy would be more successful than lowering prices?

You: Well, the reason we can pursue this strategy is that even if all our competitors lower their prices, they would be likely to attract more price-sensitive customers. Our core customer base, however, places primary focus on the service we provide, not on the price. These are the customers that The Ritz Carlton, as a luxury hotel, caters to.

Interviewer: All right. Would you offer any incentives other than the limo service and the upgrades?

You: Yes. To do this, however, we need to first understand who our target customers are so that we can offer benefits that cater to their needs. Do we know what types of customers typically stay at the hotel?

Interviewer: What would be your guess?

You: Given the nature of the hotel and location there are likely two types of customers: business professionals, and leisure vacationers. Next we need to identify which of the two segments has been affected to a larger degree by the forest fires. Do we have any information on that?

Interviewer: No.

You: Well, one way we could determine which of the two segments has been most affected is to find out whether our occupancy has been more impacted during the week or on the weekend. Do we know that?

Interviewer: Assume the weekend occupancy has declined the most.

You: That would lead me to believe that the demand from business professionals, who are likely to stay at the hotel during the week, has declined to a lesser degree than the demand from leisure vacationers. So the incentives we offer would pertain to this group.

Interviewer: Any examples?

You: Well, leisure travelers are more likely to take advantage of hotel amenities such as the spa, pools, and golf courses. So we might consider offering additional services, perhaps a golf/tennis pro and specialized massages and treatments. We could also consider offering complimentary services such as in-room massages and complimentary bottles of champagne with the bookings of some of the larger suites.

Interviewer: What about business guests of the hotel?

You: For business travelers we could offer enhanced conferencing facilities, maybe even videoconferencing. Another option is to offer additional tech support to assist with setting up Internet connection, as well as to provide support in case the customers' computer malfunctions. We could also offer additional amenities that appeal to both leisure and business travelers, such as a personal concierge or butler.

Interviewer: Great. Those are some interesting suggestions. Good luck, and have a good day.

CASE COMMENTS: The case deals with a hotel facing intense price competition caused by a decline in customer demand resulting from unfavorable environmental conditions (forest fires). Rather than engaging in a price war, the interviewee weighs the advantages and drawbacks of a price cut and determines that a better solution for enhancing the hotel's value proposition is to increase benefits rather than lower the price. Using the booking pattern (weekdays vs. weekends) as a proxy, the interviewee identifies two distinct customer segments and makes recommendations on enhancing value for each one.

External-Change Practice Cases

○ A home furnishing retailer with more than 350 store locations and catalog operations in the United States has recently been experiencing declining profits. This reverses more than 25 years of success. The company believes this to be caused by market crowding due to new competitors. As a consultant, what recommendations would you make?

○ Due to the increased pressures of social awareness and government programs on the dangers of high sugar diets, a major cereal brand has been experiencing declining sales. It is considering replacing high fructose corn syrup with Splenda, an artificial sugar, in all of its cereal products. Is this a good idea? What should it do?

○ A once dominant 40-year-old 35mm film manufacturer faces a market that has been radically changed by digital photography. Film cameras now account for only 10% of the American market. You have been hired to help the company make a plan for its future. How would you advise it?

○ A regional hardware store is trying to compete with the introduction of national competitors in its area, such as Home Depot. You have been hired to help the company address concerns that this development raises. How would you advise your client?

○ A Brazilian tire manufacturer has benefited from high tariffs on imports. Recently, because of new trade agreements, Brazil has agreed to steadily lower its tariff rate to zero over the next ten years. The tire manufacturer is very concerned about how this will impact its business, and you have been hired to help assess the situation and advise the company.

○ Our client is a small zipper manufacturer that serves a niche market. Due to the popularity of one of the bags that uses its zippers, orders for zippers are skyrocketing. Management wants to increase capacity. You have been hired to determine if this is a good idea. As a consultant, how would you advise your client?

○ A telecommunications company has sponsored professional golfing tournaments for a number of years. Because of decreasing profits, it is considering canceling its sponsorship. Should it?

○ An online computer store has been losing sales. Market analysts believe that this is due to an initiative by a major competitor to offer superior customer service. How should the company react?

○ A company that manufactures a well-known brand of potato chips has recently hired you. It is concerned about new scientific findings linking trans fatty acids (which can be found in its products) to heart disease. How would you advise your client?

o You are the CEO of a small company that makes clothing out of recycled goods. A new government law makes all goods that are made out of 100% recycled material tax-free. What actions would you take to reap the most reward from this new development?

o You are the CEO of a South African-based mining company that owns the rights for large tracts of silicon mineral deposits. Recently, a special quality has been discovered about the silicon in these sites, which makes it the only known kind in the world that can be used for super-nano computers (computer processors that are smaller than a grain of sand). Unfortunately, there is currently no demand for these devices. How would you react to this new information?

o A small U.S.-based company that specializes in making chainsaws for lumberjacks is concerned about a new bill in Congress that would turn much of America's woodlands into wildlife preserves. How should it respond to this development?

o You are the CEO of Boeing. You have a long-standing relationship with many American-based mail delivery services such as UPS, who use your cargo planes to deliver their mail. You're worried about the introduction of the new Airbus x500 cargo plane, which offers clients many more benefits than your planes at the same price. How do you react?

o In an effort to fight drug trafficking from Latin America, the U.S. government places numerous sanctions on Columbia, including the coffee trade. You have been hired by a national coffee house franchise, similar to Starbucks, to deal with the expected skyrocketing price of coffee. How would you advise the franchise?

o A toy manufacturer has gained tremendous popularity by using a flexible strain of plastic, known as flastic, in many of its products. Unfortunately, it has recently been discovered that this product is not biodegradable, and can therefore no longer be used in consumer goods. What should the company do?

Chapter Eight

Solving Company-Focused Cases

Overview

In addition to cases that deal with issues particular to a single product or service, some cases have much broader scope and deal with issues involving the entire company. To illustrate, developing a company-wide growth strategy and evaluating the viability of an acquisition or a merger exemplify common company-focused cases. Typical examples of company-focused cases are given below.

- *Develop a growth strategy for a large grocery store chain.*

- *Should Coca-Cola add ice-cream to its product mix? If yes, how should it enter the ice-cream market?*

- *Your client, a cable company, is considering entering the home security market. What is your advice?*

- *Your client has to decide whether to acquire a sports drink company. Advise your client on the viability of his acquisition strategy.*

- *Your client is trying to decide whether to acquire an office equipment company. Is this a good idea?*

- *A large credit card company is considering outsourcing some of its operations abroad. What would you advise?*

- *Your client must build a new computer chip manufacturing plant. You must decide in which country to build the plant. What factors would you consider?*

- *A local phone company is interested in diversifying into other areas besides telecommunications. It is considering entering the market for electronic home security systems. Would you recommend the company proceed with this plan?*

- *A company is considering purchasing one of two resorts. Resort A is located in the Caribbean and has an acquisition cost of $50 million while Resort B is located in Hawaii and is priced at $75 million. Which one should the company choose?*

- *An established manufacturer of mechanical pencils is considering expanding its business into other office supplies, ranging from staplers to desk disinfectants. What issues should the company consider before it expands its business?*

o   *An insurance company is thinking about acquiring a movie production studio. What factors, both internal and external, should it consider?*

o   *A diversified hedge fund is thinking about acquiring a winery in the Burgundy region of France. Your task is to help determine a fair price for the winery.*

o   *A company with an established brand of dress shoes is considering acquiring a sports watch company. What motivations are driving this decision, and what issues should the company consider before going ahead with this acquisition?*

o   *A bank in the Pacific Northwest is considering entering the brokerage business. Is this a good idea?*

o   *A fashion apparel company is thinking about expanding overseas. Should it open its own store, or sell through local distributors?*

o   *A major computer chip manufacturer is thinking about acquiring a graphic chip manufacturer. Under what circumstances is this a good idea?*

Solving Company-Focused Cases

The two most typical company-focused cases given in case interviews involve identifying a company's growth opportunities and evaluating the viability of a merger or acquisition. These two types of questions are discussed in more detail below.

Developing a Growth Strategy

Growth-strategy cases can best be solved using the *product-market growth framework* (also referred to as the Ansoff matrix). This framework identifies four distinct strategies based on the type of offering (existing vs. new) and the type of customers (current vs. new). The resulting 2 x 2 matrix contains four product-market strategies commonly referred to as (1) market penetration, (2) market development, (3) product development, and (4) diversification (Figure 1).

Figure 1. Product-Market Growth Matrix

	Current Customers	New Customers
Current Products	Market penetration	Market development
New Products	Product development	Diversification

Market-penetration aims at increasing the sales of an existing offering among a company's current customers. A common market-penetration strategy is increasing the usage rate. To illustrate, airlines stimulate demand from current customers by adopting frequent-flyer programs; packaged goods manufacturers enclose repurchase coupons as part of their product offerings; orange juice manufacturers promote drinking orange juice throughout the day rather than for breakfast only.

Market-development aims to grow sales by introducing an existing offering to new customers. In this case, the company builds on the success of its offerings to attract new customers. The two most common market-development strategies include targeting a new customer segment in an existing geographic area and introducing the offering to a different geographic area (e.g., exporting products to a new country). Market-development strategies aimed at attracting new customers include price promotions (e.g., price reductions, coupons, and rebates), new distribution channels, and communication strategies focused on different customer segment(s).

Product-development aims to grow sales by introducing a new offering targeting existing customers. In this case, the company builds on its current customer base by offering new products or services. The two most common market-development strategies include developing entirely new offerings (product innovation) or extending the current product line by modifying existing offerings (product line extension). In this context, product line extensions are often achieved by adding different sizes, forms, flavors, or colors, while preserving the core set of benefits of the original offering.

Diversification aims to grow sales by introducing new offerings to new customers. Because both the offering and the customers are new to the company, this strategy is riskier than any of the other product-market strategies. The primary rationale for diversification is to take advantage of growth opportunities in areas in which the company has no presence.

Note that market penetration and market development are growth strategies involving an existing offering. In contrast, product development and diversification are broader in scope because they go beyond the company's existing offerings.

Evaluating Viability of Mergers and Acquisitions

From a company's perspective, growth can be achieved by two means: (1) internal (also referred to as "organic") growth, in which the company relies primarily on the deployment of its own resources and (2) external growth, in which the company relies on mergers and acquisitions to achieve its goals. Because mergers and acquisitions are very common in today's business world, they are also often given as problems in case interviews.

Mergers and acquisitions describe business activities that lead to combining two (or sometimes more) companies into a single company. In the case of an acquisition, one company (the acquirer) takes over another company. In contrast, in the case of a merger, two companies, typically similar in size, agree to go forward as a single new company in which they are more or less equally represented.

Depending on the relationship between the companies, two types of mergers and acquisitions can be distinguished: vertical and horizontal. Vertical M&A involve extending the ownership upstream (toward suppliers) or downstream (toward buyers). Upstream M&A are also referred to as backward integration, whereas downstream M&A are referred to as forward integration. In contrast to vertical M&A, which occur along the supply-distribution chain, horizontal M&A typically involve companies that occupy similar positions in the value-delivery chain and often compete for the same customers.

Solving M&A cases typically involves three key steps: (1) identifying the goals underlying the proposed merger/acquisition, (2) evaluating its viability, and (3) comparing it to alternative solutions for achieving the same goal. These three steps are illustrated in Figure 2 and discussed in more detail below.

Figure 2. Solving M&A Cases

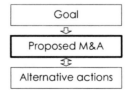

▸ Identify the goal of the M&A

Most mergers and acquisitions aim to achieve growth in cases where external opportunities present a better option than the internally available options. In this context, M&A are typically aimed at achieving economies of scale and scope, gaining competitive advantage, as well as for managerial-specific reasons. These factors are discussed in more detail below.

Economies of scale. Economies of scale reflect an inverse relationship between the scale of production and the marginal production costs, such that marginal production costs decrease with the increase in the production output. The general idea is that combining two companies will result in greater operational efficiencies and market effectiveness due to the sheer *magnitude* of their assets and operations. In other words, the logic here is that values of the two companies involved in the M&A are expected to be super-additive, creating value over and beyond the values of the individual companies (e.g., 1+1=3). Economies of scale typically can be achieved in the following areas:

- *Operation efficiencies.* Combining the operations (e.g. manufacturing and supply-chain management) of two companies often leads to greater efficiency stemming from factors such as larger scale and better coordination. For example, M&A typically lead to workforce reduction due to elimination of duplicate functions.

- *Increased channel power.* Combining two companies tends to increase their power vis-à-vis retailers and suppliers due to the concentrated purchase and sales volume.

- *Lower financial costs.* Combining two companies can also lead to a reduction in financial costs since larger firms often have an easier time raising capital and tend to have lower cost of capital than smaller companies.

Economies of scope. Economies of scope arise from *synergies* between the combined companies. The general idea here is that combining two companies will result in greater operational efficiencies due to the *complementarity* of their assets and competencies. Economies of scope typically can be achieved in the following areas:

- *Operation synergies.* Combining companies can create operational efficiencies by optimizing complementary resources and processes.

- *Greater customer-reach efficiency.* Combining companies with complementary products (e.g., banking and brokerage services) creates efficiencies for reaching new markets for each of the companies (often referred to as cross-selling).

- *Optimizing financial performance.* M&A can be used to diversify the company's product line to hedge a company's financial performance in case of a sales downturn. M&A can also be used to take advantage of certain tax benefits resulting from combining the two companies.

Gaining competitive advantage. In addition to achieving economies of scale and scope, M&A activities also can be motivated by competitive reasons.

    o *Eliminating key competitors.* By merging with or acquiring a key competitor, a company can effectively eliminate some of its strategically important competition.

    o *Acquiring scarce resources.* M&A can provide unique access to resources in short supply, such as scarce raw materials, proprietary technologies, and skilled personnel. For example, to stay on top of technological developments, medical, pharmaceutical, and high-tech companies often merge with or acquire firms with proprietary technologies.

Management-specific reasons. M&A can also be driven by factors such as management compensation (e.g., merging with or acquiring a company with a higher scale of compensation is likely to benefit the managers paid at the lower scale) or power (e.g., managing a larger company).

▸ Evaluate the viability of the proposed merger or acquisition

The evaluation of a proposed merger or acquisition involves two types of analyses: (1) evaluating the strategic implications of the merger or acquisition and (2) evaluating the financial aspect of the merger or acquisition. These two types of analyses are discussed in more detail below.

The strategic viability of a merger or acquisition can be best analyzed in the context of the 5-C framework by examining the proposed action from the viewpoint of the company, its customers, collaborators, and competitors in a particular political, social, economic, technological, and regulatory context. These five factors are outlined below.

    o *Company analysis* involves two aspects: (1) evaluating the degree to which the core competencies and strategic assets of the target will enable the company to achieve its goals (see "Strategic Asset Analysis" and "Core Competencies Analysis" following this section) and (2) evaluating the fit between the two companies (e.g., strategic fit of these companies' core competencies and strategic assets, potential synergies, culture, knowledge, and technology fit.).

    o *Customer analysis* involves evaluating the impact of the proposed action on customers' reaction to the company's offering.

    o *Collaborator analysis* involves evaluating the impact of the proposed action on a company's relationship with its collaborators, such as suppliers and distributors. Mergers and acquisitions typically strengthen the company's negotiating power vis-à-vis its collaborators due to the increase in purchase volume and the decrease in the number of competitors.

    o *Competitive analysis* involves evaluating the impact of the proposed action on the competitive dynamics in the marketplace and, in particular, competitors' reaction to the M&A activity.

    o *Context analysis* involves evaluating various political, economic, social, technological, and regulatory (e.g., anti-trust, taxation) factors on the proposed action.

The financial viability of a proposed action is a result of evaluating this action's monetary benefits and costs. A key issue in the case of mergers and acquisitions involves valuation of the target company. There are different approaches to valuation; each approach has its advantages as well as shortcomings. The most common approaches involve using benchmarks such as discounted cash flows, comparative metrics, and replacement costs.

- *Discounted cash flow (DCF)* analysis determines a company's current value according to its estimated future cash flows, discounted to a current value using the company's weighted average costs of capital.

- *Comparative metrics.* This approach determines the company's valuation based on comparable companies in the industry. Commonly used comparative metrics are price-earnings (P/E) ratios and price-sales ratios. To illustrate, comparing P/E stock ratios of companies within the same industry can serve as a benchmark for determining the P/E ratio of the target company.

- *Replacement cost.* An alternative approach to valuation involves estimating the costs to rebuild the company being acquired. The logic for this approach is that if the replacement cost is significantly lower than the asking price, instead of acquiring the target, the company can simply choose to create a new company rather than acquiring an existing one.

It is important to note that none of these approaches explicitly accounts for the potential benefits (economies of scale and scope, competitive impact) from combining the two companies. Because these factors are often the driving force for many acquisitions, they need to be a part of the valuation of the target company.

▸ Identify alternative solutions for achieving the goal

In addition to evaluating the viability of the proposed merger, it is important to identify and evaluate possible alternative solutions for achieving the company's goal. The first question is whether the goal can be achieved through "organic growth," that is, using internal resources rather than through M&A. In this context, common M&A alternatives include outsourcing, joint ventures, and franchise agreements.

Outsourcing is probably the most common M&A alternative. Unlike M&A, where the company acquires or merges with another entity, outsourcing involves entering into a contractual relationship with an outside entity, delegating it a subset of the company's (typically non-core) activities. Typical *benefits* of outsourcing include:

- Greater effectiveness due to specialization of the contractor (e.g., better and/or faster results due to specialization, learning curve effects).

- Greater cost-efficiency (e.g., due to specialization, economies of scale, lower labor costs, favorable regulatory and/or economic environment).

- Greater flexibility (e.g., lesser commitment of resources, lower exit costs).

Despite its numerous advantages, outsourcing also has a number of important *drawbacks:*

- o Loss of control (e.g., control over operations and financial performance).
- o Loss of competencies (e.g., outsourcing R&D over time tends to diminish the company's ability to innovate).
- o Competitive threat (e.g., outsourcing enables the contractor to develop a set of competencies and eventually become a competitor).

Strategic Asset Analysis

Strategic assets are resources that are essential for the success of the business in which the company operates and serve to differentiate the company from its competitors. A company's strategic assets typically include the following factors: business infrastructure, collaborator networks, human capital, intellectual property, brands, customer base, synergistic offerings, access to scarce resources, and access to capital.

○ *Business infrastructure.* There are four basic types of business infrastructure that could be considered strategic assets: (1) manufacturing infrastructure comprising the company's production facilities and equipment; (2) service infrastructure, which includes assets such as call-center facilities and customer relationship management solutions; (3) supply-chain infrastructure integrating the manufacturing and service assets into an effective and efficient value-delivery process; and (4) management infrastructure, which involves the company's business management processes.

○ *Collaborator network.* Two types of collaborator networks can be the source of a competitive advantage: vertical networks, in which collaborators are located along the supply chain (e.g., suppliers and distributors), and horizontal networks, in which collaborators are not an integral part of the company's supply chain (e.g., research and development, manufacturing, and promotion collaborators). The key to creating sustainable collaborator networks is designing offerings that deliver superior value to the company's collaborators while building relationships that result in switching costs for collaborators (e.g., integrating collaborators' systems into the company's operations).

○ *Human capital* involves factors such as the technological, operational, business, and customer expertise of the company's employees. The key to creating sustainable human capital is delivering superior value to the company's key employees and building relationships that enhance employee loyalty.

○ *Intellectual property* covers the legal entitlement attached to an intangible asset. Two types of intellectual property can be the source of a competitive advantage: (1) industrial property, which includes inventions, industrial designs, and identity marks such as trademarks, service marks, commercial names and designations, including indications of source and appellations of origin; and (2) copyright, which includes literary and artistic works such as novels, plays, films, musical works, drawings, paintings, photographs, sculptures, and architectural designs.

○ *Brands* create competitive advantage in two different ways: (1) by identifying the company and/or its offering and (2) by differentiating it from the competition. The most common brand elements include brand name, logo, symbol, character, jingle, and slogan. Using these elements, brands provide unique value to customers, the company, and its collaborators.

○ *Existing customer base* serves as a competitive advantage in two ways: (1) by facilitating the acceptance of a company's current and new offerings and (2) by impeding the acceptance of competitive products.

- o *Synergistic offerings* are a strategic asset to the degree that they facilitate customer acceptance of related company offerings. To illustrate, Windows operating system can be viewed as a strategic asset for Microsoft because it facilitates customer adoption of related software offerings.

- o *Access to scarce resources*, such as geographic locations and natural resources, is a strategic asset because it provides the company with a unique competitive advantage.

- o *Access to capital* can be considered a strategic asset in cases where it provides the company with a unique competitive advantage. To illustrate, access to capital can influence the resources at a firm's disposal to carry out its strategy: to sustain a price war, for product and/or market development, for a communication campaign.

Core Competencies Analysis

Core competencies reflect a company's ability to perform various business tasks in an efficient and effective manner and in a way that differentiates the company from its competitors. Core competencies reflect the company's expertise in specific functional areas and are a result of focused utilization of strategic assets. A company can establish a core competency in one of four key functional areas: business management, operations management, technology development, and customer management. These four areas are discussed in more detail below.

o *Business management.* Competency in business management refers to a proficiency in effectively managing business processes such as identifying business goals, designing strategies and tactics to achieve these goals, and implementing the company's business plan. Business management competency also involves the company's ability to build the collaborator network required for the efficient functioning of the business (e.g., relationships with suppliers and distributors). This competency typically leads to strategic benefits such as business model leadership. To illustrate, Dell's core competency in business management resulted in a direct distribution business model that was one of the key reasons for its success. Other examples of companies with demonstrated competency in business management include McDonalds, Blockbuster, Starbucks, Wal-Mart, and Amazon.com.

o *Operations management.* Competency in operations management refers to an expertise in supply-chain management. Companies with competency in operations management are proficient in optimizing the effectiveness and cost-efficiency of the business processes. This competency typically leads to the strategic benefit of cost leadership in the marketplace. To illustrate, Wal-Mart's competency in operations management is reflected in its dominant position as the low-cost player in the market. Other examples of companies with demonstrated competency in operations management include Southwest Airlines, Costco, and Home Depot.

o *Technology development.* Competency in technology development refers to a company's ability to design new technological solutions. This competency typically leads to the strategic benefit of technological leadership. Examples of companies that have demonstrated competency in developing new technologies include Motorola, BASF, Google, and Intel. Note that a competency in developing new technologies does not necessarily imply a competency in developing commercially successful products. To illustrate, Xerox and its Palo Alto Research Center (PARC) have invented numerous new technologies, such as photocopying, laser printing, graphical user interface, client/server architecture, and the Ethernet, but have been slow in converting these technologies into commercial products.

o *Customer value management.* Competency in customer value management refers to expertise in understanding, creating, and managing customer value. There are three common aspects of competency in customer value management: product management, service management, and brand management. These three aspects of a firm's competency in customer value management are discussed in more detail below.

▫ *Product management.* Competency in product management refers to a company's ability to develop products that deliver superior customer value. This competency typically leads to the strategic benefit of product leadership. Examples of companies with demonstrated competency in product management include Microsoft, Merck, Apple, and Palm. Note that competency in product management is not contingent on the company's also having competency in technology management. In fact, technologically inferior products delivering need-based functionality are often more successful than technologically superior products that fail to meet customer needs. To illustrate, TiVo, the pioneer in digital video recording, exemplifies a company with competency in developing a successful product based on an existing MPEG-2 digital-encoding technology. Similarly, building on existing Internet technologies, Sling Media developed Slingbox – a user-friendly product enabling customers to watch their home TV programming from any networked computer anywhere in the world.

▫ *Service management.* Competency in service management refers to a company's ability to develop services that deliver superior customer value. This competency typically leads to the strategic benefit of service leadership. Examples of companies with demonstrated competency in service management include Ritz-Carlton, American Express, and Nordstrom.

▫ *Brand management.* Competency in brand management refers to a company's ability to build strong brands that deliver superior customer value. This competency typically leads to the strategic benefit of brand leadership. Examples of companies with demonstrated competency in brand management include Harley-Davidson, Nike, Procter & Gamble, and PepsiCo.

Company-Focused Case Examples

Company Acquisition (Caribbean Resort Case)

Interviewer: A company is considering purchasing a Caribbean resort. What factors would you consider in order to decide whether they should proceed?

You: Interesting problem... Well, first of all, what is the goal of the purchase?

Interviewer: What goals do you think a company could pursue with such a purchase?

You: One reason for this purchase could be that a company is attempting to add or increase its presence in these locations.

Interviewer: Why would a company do this?

You: There are several possible reasons. First, these might be locations with higher than usual profit margins, such that...

Interviewer: Okay, what else?

You: Second, the company might also aim to fill a gap in its product line...

Interviewer: What do you mean by this? How is it different from going after higher profit margins?

You: For example, the company might already have a presence in these locations at some but not all price points. The company might be focused on the lower end of the market while the new acquisition targets the higher end of the market, such as the luxury and super-luxury vacation resorts.

Interviewer: Is this the only way a company might want to close a gap in its product line?

You: Well, the example of the luxury resort describes a vertical line extension. A company might also consider adding a horizontal extension that is at the same price point as its existing resorts but offers a different set of benefits.

Interviewer: Could you give me an example?

You: Sure. For example, a traditional hotel chain might want to add a time-share property that involves weekly occupancy based on fractional ownership. Or, alternatively, the company might consider acquiring an all-inclusive family-oriented resort.

Interviewer: Okay. Let's go back to the original question. Is there any other reason that a company might consider acquiring another company?

You: Well, by expanding, a company might be able to achieve certain economies of scale such as greater efficiency in operations as well as in marketing.

Interviewer: Anything else? Is there any other reason that a hotel might consider acquiring another hotel?

You: Another possibility is to take advantage of potential synergies between its existing hotels and the newly acquired resorts.

Interviewer: Could you elaborate on this?

You: Sure. For example, if the company's hotels cater to business customers, they could promote the newly acquired resort to these customers in a very effective and cost-efficient manner. Essentially, the company now will be able to provide a different type of service – a destination resort – for its current customers.

Interviewer: So, what is a destination resort?

You: Unlike typical hotels that provide lodging to travelers who have to spend time at a particular location for reasons other than the amenities/services offered by the hotel, destination hotels/resorts are usually the primary purpose of the travel – for example, beach, ski, and golf resorts. In fact, hotels we are considering acquiring are likely to be destination resorts.

Interviewer: Any other reasons why this company might consider an acquisition?

You: Another reason for the acquisition is to preempt the competition. For example, if the resort we are considering acquiring is strategically located, its acquisition by a large competitor could seriously hinder the company's operations and/or growth prospects.

Interviewer: Can you think of any other reason for the proposed acquisition?

You: Yet another reason could be the company's desire to diversify its operations. As a matter of fact, the acquiring company might not even be in the hotel business. In this context, the acquisition might be driven by the need for diversification to hedge against an eventual downturn in the industry in which the company operates.

Interviewer: Good. Can you think of reasons for diversification in the case that the acquiring company is already in the hotel business?

You: Sure. One possibility would be to ensure a more consistent, and therefore more predictable, revenue stream. For example, adding a timeshare to a hotel is likely to result in less volatile revenue stream.

Interviewer: Any other benefits of diversification in this case?

You: Well, by virtue of its location, a newly acquired resort could appeal to a different customer segment. For example, the new resort might cater to a different demographic with a demand cycle that is complementing the demand pattern of the company's current customers.

Interviewer: Good. This will do for now. We'll be in touch.

CASE COMMENTS: The case presents a scenario in which a company has to evaluate the viability of a proposed acquisition, in this case a Caribbean resort. The interviewee approaches this decision by assessing goals that a company might achieve through this action, such as increasing presence, filling in product line gaps (both vertical and horizontal), achieving greater efficiency through economies of scale, synergies, preempting competition, and diversifying its operations.

Company Acquisition (Asphalt Manufacturer Case)

Interviewer: Your client is considering acquiring a small asphalt manufacturing firm. What factors would you take into account in order to decide whether it should go ahead?

You: Well, I would first try to identify the client's motivation for the acquisition. For example, if the client's company is in a business that involves similar inputs, processes, or outputs, the goal of the acquisition might be to achieve operational synergies. If the client's company is also an asphalt manufacturer, then the acquisition goal might be to achieve economies of scale, such as more efficient operations and greater power over suppliers due to concentrated purchases. All of this should translate to lower costs, which in turn will give the client greater pricing flexibility and ultimately greater profitability.

Interviewer: Good, let's say that the client is also an asphalt manufacturer and its goal is to improve profitability by achieving greater economies of scale. So what would you do next to determine the viability of the proposed acquisition?

You: Well, I would next evaluate the impact of the proposed acquisition on the following key factors: the company, its customers, competitors, and collaborators, such as suppliers and distributors. I would also examine the impact of the political, economic, and regulatory environment on the proposed acquisition.

Interviewer: Good, walk me through these factors.

You: Sure. Let's start with evaluating the impact of the acquisition on the company. I would consider three key aspects. First, I would evaluate the core competencies and strategic assets of the client's company, as well as its overall performance in terms of revenues, costs, profit margins, and market share. Then, I would conduct a similar analysis of the target company. Finally, I would evaluate the fit between the two companies in terms of the complementarity of their core competencies and strategic assets, as well as potential economies of scale and synergies.

Interviewer: Okay. So what kind of strategic assets would you consider? Give me an example.

You: Sure. For example, business infrastructure, such as the asphalt manufacturing facilities; their existing supplier and distributor framework; the current management team; the company's image and reputation; and their existing customer base.

Interviewer: Good. So what's next?

You: Well, next I would examine who the customers and end-users of asphalt products are, their needs and preferences, as well as their projected demand for the company's products. I would also examine the key factors that are important in purchasing asphalt products: in particular, the role of manufacturing scale, availability of multiple locations, reliability, and price.

Interviewer: Who do you think are the likely customers of an asphalt company?

You: Well, come to think of it, the most likely customers would be the municipal, state, and federal government. Real estate development companies and individual contractors are likely customers as well. For the government, the price as well as the availability of multiple locations could be the key decision factors. For real estate developers and individual contractors, reliability and on-time-delivery are likely to be among the key factors.

Interviewer: You also mentioned evaluating the competition. What would you look for?

You: First, I would identify the major competitors in the markets that the client and the target company serve. I would also evaluate their core competencies and strategic assets vis-à-vis those of the client and the target company. I would also evaluate the barriers to entry to anticipate potential entry by new competitors. Another issue worth consideration is how competitors would react to the proposed acquisition.

Interviewer: Good. What other factors would you consider?

You: I would also examine the client's relationship with its suppliers and the impact of the proposed acquisition on these relationships. For instance, the proposed acquisition is likely to increase the client's negotiating power vis-à-vis its suppliers by virtue of increased purchase volume. If volume-based price reductions are possible, it might be worthwhile to quantify the expected cost savings when evaluating the financial aspect of the viability of the proposed acquisition.

Interviewer: Anything else you think your client should consider?

You: I think it would also be important to consider the overall environment in which this industry operates. This involves a variety of regulatory factors such as anti-trust legislation, labor laws, as well as local regulations concerning bidding for government contracts – including preferential treatment of minority-owned and/or women-owned businesses. Evaluating the overall state of the economy would also be pertinent to forecasting the overall industry growth.

Interviewer: Good. Let's say that the client has decided that this acquisition is strategically viable. How would you go about determining the fair acquisition price?

You: Well, one approach is to rely on a discounted cash flow analysis, which is based on the estimated future cash flows discounted to the current value, using the company's weighted cost of capital.

Interviewer: Is there any other approach the company could use?

You: Yes. Another approach is to compare the value of the to-be-acquired company to similar companies in the same industry.

Interviewer: And if no information about comparable companies is available?

You: In that case, the company can estimate the costs to rebuild the to-be-acquired company from scratch and use this as a benchmark for evaluating the feasibility of the acquisition price.

Interviewer: Is there anything else that the client should consider before going ahead with the acquisition?

You: It is also important to consider the availability of viable alternatives to the proposed acquisition that could enable the client to achieve its goals. Such alternatives might include building, rather than acquiring, additional asphalt manufacturing facilities, acquiring a different company, or creating a joint venture.

Interviewer: Good. Now let's move on to something else.

CASE COMMENTS: This case deals with assessing the viability of an acquisition, in this instance, an asphalt manufacturer. The interviewee approaches this problem by first assessing goals that the company might achieve through this action and then proceeds to evaluate the benefits and costs of the proposed acquisition by assessing the benefits and costs in terms of the company, its customers, competitors, collaborators, and context (the 5-C framework).

Company-Focused Practice Cases

○ A Japanese auto-parts manufacturer plans a market entry in the United States. What factors should it consider in order to implement its goal?

○ A French-based wine manufacturing company is looking to expand globally by acquiring a Portugal-based wine manufacturing firm. What points should it consider when assessing this decision?

○ A construction firm based in China wants to expand into a growing U.S. regional market. However, it is concerned about the impression that its construction material is of lower quality than that of U.S. firms. You have been hired to help this company construct a marketing scheme to successfully introduce this company to the U.S. market. How would you advise the company?

○ Unilever's Table Spreads operating company was considering buying the Land O' Lakes brand of butter. Only the brand name and formulas are included in this deal. Analysts believe that this is a good decision from a financial perspective. From a strategic point of view, is this a good idea?

○ A major pharmaceutical company has been approached by a small hospital that has developed a successful method to treat patients suffering from a rare muscle disorder. Since this hospital is too small to develop and market this procedure, it would like to license its program to the pharmaceutical company. What factors should the pharmaceutical company consider when making a decision about this offer?

○ A domestic telephone company is interested in diversifying and buying a cable company. It believes that there are many plausible synergies that will result from this acquisition, such as shared technology and an expanded customer base for both companies. This company has hired you to help determine a fair price for the cable company. As a consultant, how would you advise the company?

○ Our client is a cement manufacturer in Brazil that is considering adding capacity. Should it increase the scale of its current plant or build a new plant in Buenos Aires, an area undergoing a great deal of construction?

○ A major grocery store chain based in the Midwest is considering offering an Internet delivery service in order to increase the number of customers that buy its products. There are currently three competing grocery store chains in the region, though none have an Internet service. You have been hired by the company to help determine whether this idea will be profitable. How would you advise your client?

○ Our client is a large American hydraulic press manufacturer who dominates market share in the U.S. It has little international presence however, and is considering entering the German market, which it believes to be very attractive. Is this a good idea, and what issues should it consider?

o A not-for-profit hospital currently operates at a $15 million dollar loss every year. At this rate, its endowment will be gone in three years and operations will have to end. How can you help save the hospital from closing its doors?

o A Malaysian electronics company manufactures affordable stereo systems. It is considering expanding its operations to Japan. What are the relevant issues that this company should consider when assessing this decision?

o A fast food restaurant is considering purchasing a large national meat-processing company to supply all of its locations with fresh hamburger meat. Currently, the restaurant buys its meats from regional butchers. What factors should this company consider before going ahead with the acquisition?

o An office furniture manufacturer is thinking about adding capacity by building a new manufacturing plant in the Philippines. Is this a good idea?

o A paper manufacturer is considering acquiring woodlands in Brazil. What factors should it consider in making this decision?

o Your client is an established international health care company that specializes in developing medical equipment and has relationships with hospitals and clinics around the world. It is considering purchasing a California-based software company that claims to have developed a state-of-the-art logistical software that would help hospitals coordinate their activities. You have been hired to asses the benefits of this acquisition. How would you do this?

o A water-purifying company is thinking about buying an alcohol distilling plant. What motivation could be behind this decision?

o Your client is a company with a discount brand of soda called Fizzle Pop. The product is typically distributed in grocery stores across the country, but over the last several years, the company has noticed that the product does best in Wal-Mart. You have been hired to help the company make some changes to accommodate these new findings. How would you advise this company?

o An established American brand of jeans is facing increased pressure by designer clothing retailers. The company is considering diversifying into other areas of apparel to counteract the loss of market share it has experienced in the last several years. What issues should the company consider when assessing this decision?

o A laundry detergent company is considering buying an air freshener company in order to use its familiar scents in its products. You have been hired by the client to determine how customers of both companies might react to this move. How would you advise the company?

o Home Depot wants to increase its market share by targeting the married woman market with its house improvement products. In order to do this the company wants to revamp its image and create a new marketing scheme. You have been hired to help implement these plans. How would you advise your client?

Chapter Nine

Analyzing Cases with Pre-Identified Solutions

Overview

Cases with pre-identified solutions are very similar to cases without proposed solutions discussed in the earlier chapters. The key difference is that a potential solution is readily available and its viability needs to be explicitly evaluated. To illustrate, a case might involve evaluating the viability of launching an aggressive advertising campaign to promote a new offering, evaluating the viability of introducing monetary incentives to increase the market share of a product line, as well as determining the viability of a company's decision to lower prices in response to a new competitive entry. Typical examples of cases with pre-identified solutions are given below.

- *Your client is considering launching a new product. Market data show that launching the product will decrease sales of an existing product by x%. Do you launch the product?*

- *To increase its subscriber base, TiVo is considering giving a TiVo recorder to each customer who signs a two-year contract. What would you advise?*

- *Your client, a large soft drink manufacturer, is considering switching from glass to plastic bottles. Is this a good idea?*

- *A car manufacturer is considering reducing prices to gain market share. What do you tell him?*

- *A fast-food chain is considering lowering prices to improve its bottom line. Is this a good idea?*

- *A small software company is considering launching its new product by advertising during the Super Bowl. What would be your advice?*

- *Your client, a major online content provider, is considering introducing a new pricing structure, which implies annual price increases. Is this a good idea?*

- *Your client is considering raising the price of its bestselling product in order to meet its profit goals. Is this a good idea?*

- *A major European airline is thinking about lowering its fares to better compete with discount carriers. Is this a good idea?*

○ *Company X wants to increase the market share of its flagship product so that it can claim that its product has the largest customer base. What would you advise so that the company can reach its goal?*

○ *An upscale ice-cream manufacturer is considering buying a fleet of refrigeration trucks to establish its own distribution system. Is this a good idea?*

○ *A solar panel manufacturer is contemplating adding capacity. Is this a good idea?*

Analyzing Cases with Pre-Identified Solutions

Because they are typically variations of cases without readily proposed solutions, cases with pre-identified solutions usually fall into one of the following three categories: action-planning, performance-gap, and external-change cases. Each of these cases, discussed in more detail below, can concern either a particular offering or the entire company.

Analyzing Action-Planning Cases with Pre-Identified Solutions

Action-planning cases with pre-identified solutions are typically solved using the following three-step algorithm (Figure 1).

o Identify the *goal* to be achieved by the proposed action.

o Evaluate the ability of the *proposed action* to achieve the company's goal. Identify the specifics of the proposed action and its strengths (benefits) and weaknesses (costs) with respect to achieving the goal.

o Evaluate the proposed action vis-à-vis the *alternative actions*. Identify the alternative actions that will also enable the company to achieve the company's goal and evaluate the relative advantages and disadvantages of the proposed action vis-à-vis the alternative actions.

Figure 1. Analyzing Action-Planning Cases with Pre-identified Solutions

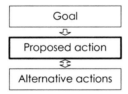

Analyzing Problem-Solving Cases with Pre-Identified Solutions

Problem-solving cases with pre-identified solutions are typically analyzed following the four steps outlined below (Figure 2).

o Identify the *problem* to be solved by the proposed action.

o Identify the *cause* of the problem.

o Evaluate the ability of the *proposed action* to eliminate the cause, thus solving the problem.

o Evaluate the proposed solution vis-à-vis the *alternative actions*.

Figure 2. Analyzing Problem-Solving Cases with Pre-identified Solutions

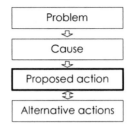

Analyzing External-Change Cases with Pre-identified Solutions

External-change cases with pre-identified solutions are typically solved using the following four-step approach (Figure 3).

o Identify the *external change* to be addressed by the proposed action.

o Identify the *impact* of this change on the company's performance.

o Evaluate the ability of the *proposed action* to mitigate the impact of the external change (when the change poses a threat) or to optimize the company's chances to take advantage of the external change (when the change presents an opportunity).

o Evaluate the proposed response vis-à-vis the *alternative actions*. Identify the alternative responses to the external change and evaluate the relative advantages and disadvantages of the proposed response vis-à-vis the alternative responses.

Figure 3. Analyzing External-Change Cases with Pre-identified Solutions

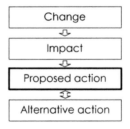

Practice Cases with Pre-Identified Solutions

○ A major airline is considering adding a route from New York to Shanghai. What might be motivating this decision, and what issues should the company consider before introducing this route?

○ Burger King is considering offering healthy food items, such as salads and fruit bowls, in the U.S. Should it go ahead with this idea?

○ An established restaurant that is famous for its fried chicken is considering launching a retail version of the company's signature chicken breading so that customers can make fried chicken at home. What factors should the company consider when determining whether or not to go ahead with this plan?

○ Our client is a major U.S. auto services chain that has over 150 store locations in the Midwest. Management, however, is concerned that the market in this area is saturated and wants to expand to new locations. You have been hired by the company to help determine an optimal course of action. As a consultant how would you advise the client?

○ A producer of consumer plastic, Tupperware, is considering making a $2 million investment to upgrade some process equipment. Would you recommend that it go ahead with this project? Why or why not?

○ While interest in opera seems to be on the rise, The Royal Opera Company has just suffered its third straight year of profit loss. It believes the cause is the relatively high marketing budget and has plans to make cuts. As a consultant, what recommendations can you make?

○ A retailer with 25 stores located in shopping malls in metropolitan and suburban centers has been experiencing slower than expected growth. Profits are also down, despite major cost-cutting initiatives. Management plans to close stores and cut costs further. What might the problem be, and how should it be addressed?

○ Cool Whip has an 80% share of the whipped cream market. With low production costs and high margins, it is a very profitable product. However, over the last several years, sales of the product have been flat despite aggressive advertising campaigns. Management believes that sales have peaked and wants to cut the marketing budget. Is this a good idea?

○ A fruit juice producer has packaged juice for retail locations in 16-ounce carton containers for several years. Acting on the recommendation of consultants, the producer plans to purchase a machine that packages the juice in 8-ounce cans. You have been hired by the company to determine whether it should go ahead with this plan. How would you advise the client?

○ A company is considering purchasing one of two profitable cruise lines. Option 1 operates in the Caribbean and has an initial cost of $40 million. Option 2 operates off the coast of Alaska and has an initial cost of $20 million. The company has an ROA of 15%. Which line should the company purchase and why?

o Our client is a large clothing retailer that has been losing market share to discounters. The client plans to address this problem by launching a discount store associated with its brand. As a consultant, what advice would you have for the company regarding this decision?

o An infant formula manufacturer that has a relatively small market share would like to grow its share while maintaining profitability. How should it work towards this goal?

o A battery manufacturer makes products that are superior in quality and lifetime to its competitors. However, it has recently been experiencing declining profits. The manufacturer plans to cut funding to their research team, which is one of the highest sources of cost for the company. What issues should it consider before going ahead with this decision?

o A major distributor of prune-related products is considering a new advertising campaign to market its goods to a younger audience. How should it execute this plan?

o A major brand of hotels has entered into talks with the maker of a revolutionary waterbed that has been on the market for several years. Though these beds are met with almost universal approval by all who try them, they have very little market penetration. The idea is that the waterbeds would be installed in each hotel room free of charge, but the hotel would be responsible for marketing these beds to its customers. What factors should the hotel consider when assessing this proposal?

o The clothing retailer Gap has noticed that an untapped but lucrative market is in fashion accessories aimed exclusively at middle-aged men. It is therefore considering launching a new store aimed exclusively at this segment. You have been hired to help execute this plan. How would you advise the client?

o A brand of luxury hotels with a worldwide presence is considering adding a timeshare option at its most exclusive locations in order to boost sales. You have been hired to assess the feasibility of this proposal. As a consultant, what recommendations would you have for the company?

o Harley Davidson believes that there is a large market for its motorcycles in Asia. What factors should it consider when introducing its products to this market?

o A Korean maker of LCD computer monitors wants to get into the LCD television industry. You have been hired by the company to help implement this plan. How would you advise your client?

Essential Strategic Concepts

Backward Integration: A form of *vertical integration* that involves upstream expansion of the supply chain.

Brand Equity: The monetary value of the brand.

Brand Extension: The strategy of using the same brand name in a different context (e.g., different product category or different price tier). There are two main types of brand extensions: within-category extensions and cross-category extensions. In within-category brand extensions, the same brand name is applied to several products within the same product category. In contrast, in cross-category brand extensions, the same brand name is applied to products in different categories. To illustrate, extending the Starbucks name to different coffee flavors is typically referred to as a within-category (or line-based) brand extension; whereas, extending it to ice cream is considered a cross-category brand extension.

Cannibalization: Scenario in which a newly introduced offering steals share from other offering(s) within the same company. To illustrate, the introduction of Vanilla Coke cannibalized the sales of Coca-Cola Classic. Cannibalization is not necessarily "bad" for the company. In many cases, cannibalization can have an overall positive impact (e.g., when the margins of the new offering are higher than that of the cannibalized one, or when the new offering seeks to achieve different strategic goals).

Captive Pricing: see *complementary pricing*.

Category Killers: Specialty retailers that focus on one product category such as electronics or business supplies at very competitive prices (e.g., Home Depot, Office Depot, CompUSA, PETsMART).

Channel Conflict: Tension between members of a *distribution channel,* often caused by different profit optimization strategies of each channel member. There are three types of channel conflicts: *vertical, horizontal,* and *multichannel.*

Channel Power: The ability of one channel member to get another channel member to do what it otherwise would not have done (e.g., a retailer allocating premium shelf space to a given manufacturer's products without being explicitly compensated for it).[1]

Co-branding: Joint marketing strategy that involves using multiple brand names in a single offering (e.g., United Airlines Mileage Plus Visa credit card, Nike Air Jordan products).

Competitive-Parity Budgeting: Marketing strategy based on (1) matching the competitors' absolute level of spending or (2) the proportion per point of market share.

Complementary Pricing: Pricing strategy applicable to uniquely compatible, multi-part offerings, whereby a company charges a low (relative to its cost) introductory price on the first part and higher prices for the other parts. Classic examples include razors and blades, printers and cartridges, cell phones and cell phone service. Note that the unique compatibility is crucial to the success of complementary pricing: Only the printer manufacturer should be able to sell cartridges that fit in its printers (also known as *two-part pricing, captive pricing*).

Consumer Promotions: Promotional activities aimed at the consumer (rather than the retailer). Typical consumer promotional activities include free samples, coupons, and rebates.

Cost-Plus Pricing: A pricing method in which the final price is determined by adding a fixed mark-up to the cost of the product. It is easy to calculate and is commonly used in industries where profit margins are relatively stable. Its key drawback is that it does not take into account customer demand and competitive pricing.

Customer Equity: The lifetime value of a particular customer to a company.

Direct Channel: Distribution strategy in which the manufacturer and the end-customer interact directly with each other without intermediaries (see also *indirect channel* and *hybrid channel*).

Diversification: A market growth strategy aimed at developing offerings that are new to the company and introducing those offerings to customers not currently served by the company (see *product-market growth matrix*).

Economies of Scale: An inverse relationship between the scale of production and the marginal production costs. Thus, if the marginal production costs do not vary as a function of the output volume, there are no economies of scale. If, however, marginal production costs decrease with the increase in the production output, then this increase reflects the economies of scale. By the same logic, if an increase in the production output results in an increase in the marginal production costs, then this decrease reflects diseconomies of scale. Therefore, for a given company, the marginal production costs decrease until they reach a certain minimum (economies of scale), then increase as the firm size increases further (diseconomies of scale).

Everyday Low Pricing (EDLP): Pricing strategy whereby a retailer maintains low prices without frequent price promotions.

Experience Curve: The curve describing how costs of production decline as cumulative output increases over time. The concept was introduced by the Boston Consulting Group in 1966 to describe the finding that costs decline approximately 20 to 30% in real terms each time accumulated experience doubles.[2] At present, the term "experience curve" is used in a more general sense to capture the notion that costs tend to decrease with experience. Often used interchangeably with *learning curve*.

Experience Curve Pricing: Pricing strategy based on an anticipated future lower cost structure resulting from scale economies and experience curve effects.

Extension: A strategy whereby a company adds a new offering to its current product line, thus extending the assortment of its products and services. The key reason for extending an existing offering is to develop a new value proposition to better address the needs of a specific customer segment. Two types of extensions are commonly distinguished: *horizontal* and *vertical*.

Fighting Brand: Strategic (most often downscale) product extension to confront lower priced competitor(s).

Forward Buying: Increasing the channel inventory (also referred to as "channel stuffing"), usually to take advantage of a manufacturer's promotion and/or in anticipation of price increases.

Forward Integration: A form of *vertical integration* that involves downstream expansion of the supply chain (e.g., a manufacturer establishing its own distribution system).

Heterogeneous Market: A scenario in which customers vary in their response to a company's offering (see also *homogeneous market*).

Homogeneous Market: A scenario in which all customers are likely to react in a similar manner with respect to a company's offering (e.g., they like the same combination of product and service features, are willing to pay a similar price for a given offering, are likely to respond to a company's promotional activities in a similar manner, can be reached through the same communication means, have access to the offering through the same distribution channels, etc.) See also *heterogeneous market*.

Horizontal Channel Conflict: A conflict between members within the same level of the channel (e.g., between two retailers). Horizontal conflicts occur when different channels target the same customer segment with identical or substitutable offerings (e.g., different retailers selling the same product to the same customer). See also *channel conflict*.

Horizontal Extension: An *extension* in which the price is not the key differentiating factor between the original and the extended offering (Figure 1). To illustrate, different yogurt flavors and different types of cola (regular, cherry, vanilla, diet, caffeine-free) would be considered horizontal extensions. See also *extension, vertical extension*.

Figure 1. Horizontal Extension

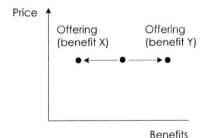

Hybrid Channel: Distribution strategy in which the manufacturer and the end-customer interact with each other through multiple channels – for example, directly and through intermediaries such as wholesalers and/or retailers (see also *direct channel* and *indirect channel*).

Image Pricing: see *price signaling*.

Indirect Channel: Distribution strategy in which the manufacturer and the end-customer interact with each other through intermediaries such as wholesalers and/or retailers (see also *direct channel* and *hybrid channel*).

Learning Curve: The curve describing how labor costs of production decline as cumulative output increases over time. The logic behind the concept of a learning curve is that labor hours per unit decline on repetitive tasks. The term learning curve is often used interchangeably with the more general concept of experience curve, although an argument has been made to differentiate the two concepts.[3]

Loss Leadership: Pricing strategy that involves setting a low price (often at or below cost) in an attempt to increase the sales of other products and services (e.g., a retailer sets the price low on a popular item in an attempt to build store traffic, thus increasing the sales of other, more profitable items).

Market Potential: Maximum total of sales of a product/service by all firms.

Marketing Mix: A cumulative description of the key components of marketing tactics: product, service, brand, price, incentives, communications, and distribution. Also referred to as the Four Ps: product, price, promotion, and place.

Marketing Plan: The marketing plan is an outline of the key aspects of managing a company's offering. Most marketing plans have the following structure: (1) executive summary, (2) description of the company's objectives, (3) overview of the company's strategy, (4) overview of the company's marketing mix variables, (5) implementation plan, (6) evaluation and control benchmarks, and (7) various background analyses that include all supporting information.

Merchandisers: Indirect sales force that offers support to retailers for in-store activities such as shelf location, pricing, and compliance with special programs.

Niche Strategy: Marketing strategy aimed at a distinct and relatively small customer segment.

Opportunity Analysis: Strategic process of evaluating the environment in which the company operates with the purpose of identifying opportunities for developing a new offering or optimizing existing offerings.

Parallel Importing: The practice of importing products from a country in which the price is lower into a country in which the same product is priced higher. A hypothetical example of this practice would be importing drugs from Canada to the United States. In most cases, parallel importing is illegal in the United States.

Pareto Principle: The 80/20 relationship discovered in the late 1800s by the economist Vilfredo Pareto.[4] Pareto established that 80% of the land in Italy was owned by 20% of the population. He later observed that 20% of the peapods in his garden yielded 80% of the peas that were harvested. The Pareto Principle, or the 80/20 Rule, has proven its validity in a number of other areas. In marketing, the most common illustration of the 80/20 rule is that 80% of revenues are likely to be generated by 20% of customers (or products).

Path of Least Resistance: Efficiency-based hierarchy of marketing strategies to increase sales. For most companies, the path of least resistance implies that it is most efficient to increase sales by starting with current customers, then by luring competitors' customers, and finally by building demand for the entire category. One exception concerns market leaders who are more likely to benefit from building category demand than from trying to steal share from a niche competitor.

Penetration Pricing: Pricing strategy aimed at rapidly gaining market share. This strategy often leads to higher sales volume, albeit at lower margins (see also *price skimming*).

Positioning: Positioning reflects how the company wants its offering to be perceived by the customer; it is the process of creating a distinct image of a company's offering in a customer's mind. Positioning involves prioritizing an offering's existing benefits and costs in order to highlight its key distinctive benefits. Thus, Volvo positions its cars as the safest vehicles on the road, Apple emphasizes the user-friendliness of its products, and Gillette promotes its razors as "the best a man can get."

Positioning Statement: An internal document that offers a succinct summary of a company's targeting and positioning strategy. The positioning statement identifies three main aspects of an offering's strategy: (1) target customers, (2) frame of reference (i.e., the reference point used by customers to evaluate the offering), and (3) the primary benefit(s), (i.e., the key reason to buy and/or use the offering). Depending on the frame of reference, two types of positioning statements can be identified: non-comparative, which define the key benefit of the offering relative to customer needs without explicitly comparing the offering to the other offerings in the market (Figure 2), and comparative, which define the offering's key benefit by explicitly relating it to competitive offerings (Figure 3).

Figure 2. Non-Comparative Positioning Statement

.... is the best ....
           (offering)   (product category)

for ....
                           (target market)

because ....
                    (unique value proposition)

Figure 3. Comparative Positioning Statement

.... is a better ....
           (offering)   (product category)

than ....
                        (competitive offering)

for ....
                           (target market)

because ....
                    (unique value proposition)

Predatory Pricing: A strategy that involves selling below cost with the intent of driving competitors out of business. In most cases, predatory pricing is illegal in the United States.

Prestige Pricing: Pricing strategy whereby the price is set at a relatively high level for the purpose of creating an exclusive image of the offering.

Price Discrimination: A strategy that involves charging different buyers different prices for goods of equal grade and quality.

Price Fixing: A practice in which competitors conspire to set prices for a given product and/or service. In most cases, price fixing is illegal in the United States.

Price Signaling: (1) Pricing strategy that aims to capitalize on price-quality inferences (i.e., higher priced products are also likely to be higher quality). Primarily used when the actual product benefits are not readily observable (also known as *prestige pricing*); (2) Indirect communication (direct price collusion is prohibited by law) between companies, aimed at indicating their intentions with respect to their pricing strategy.

Price Skimming: Pricing strategy in which a firm sets a high initial price in order to maximize profit margins, usually at the expense of market share (see also *penetration pricing*).

Private Label: Branding strategy in which an offering is branded by the retailer (e.g., Kenmore – Sears' brand for home appliances, Kirkland – Costco's private brand). Private labels are often contrasted to national brands, which are branded by the manufacturer or a third party rather than by the retailer (e.g., Coca-Cola, IBM, and Nike). Typically, private labels tend to be less expensive than the national brands although there are many exceptions, such as private labels offered by up-scale retailers (e.g., Nordstrom, Marks & Spenser).

Product Line Extension: see *extension.*

Product-Line Pricing: Pricing strategy whereby the price of each individual offering is determined as a function of the offering's place in the relevant product line (e.g., the price of BMW's 3-series models is a function of the prices of its 5- and 7-series models).

Product-Market Growth Matrix: A 2 (offering: existing vs. new) x 2 (market: existing vs. new) matrix advanced by Igor Ansoff[5] outlining the four key market growth strategies: market penetration, market development, product development, and diversification.

Promotional Allowance: Trade promotion offered as a reward for conducting promotional activities on behalf of the manufacturer. Typical forms of promotional allowance involve an advertising allowance, in which retailers are given a discount in exchange for promoting a product in their own advertisements, and a slotting allowance given to retailers to allocate shelf space for a new product.

Psychographics: Individual differences represented by personality and lifestyle traits (e.g., activities, interests, and opinions). Most often used in segmentation and targeting decisions.

Pull Strategy: The practice of creating demand for a company's offering by promoting the offering directly to end-users, who in turn demand the offering from intermediaries, ultimately "pulling" the offering through the channel (Figure 4). To illustrate, the manufacturer might extensively advertise its products and services to the end-users and/or promote its offerings through direct mail, coupons, contests, etc.

Figure 4. Pull Strategy

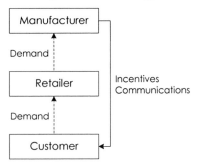

Push Strategy: The practice of creating demand for a company's product by offering incentives to channel members, who in turn push the product downstream to end-users (Figure 5). To illustrate, the manufacturer might offer high margins on their products and services so that retailers have a vested interest in selling the product. In the same vein, the manufacturer might educate a retailer's sales force about the benefits of its offerings and provide the retailer with promotional materials, thus facilitating the sales process.

Figure 5. Push Strategy

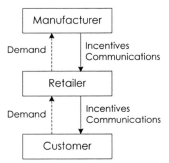

Repositioning: A change in the positioning of a given offering. The key reason for repositioning is to change the existing value proposition to better address the needs of target customers, the company, and/or its collaborators.

Reverse Engineering: The process of analyzing competitors' products (often by physically taking them apart) to learn about design characteristics, manufacturing processes, and materials.

Reverse Logistics: The process of reclaiming recyclable and reusable materials, and returns for repair, remanufacturing, or disposal.

Segmentation: The process of dividing buyers into groups with similar characteristics (e.g., needs, age, and income). Segmentation is based on the idea that because customers in a given segment respond in a similar manner to a company's offering, they can be treated as if they were a single entity and their needs can be served by the same offering. Thus, through segmentation the company can reduce the diversity (or heterogeneity) in the marketplace by focusing on a relatively small number of segments. Note that dividing the marketplace into separate segments is highly subjective and is likely to vary depending on the segmentation criteria. A good segmentation should yield segments that are mutually exclusive and collectively exhaustive: they should be sufficiently different from one another so that they do not overlap and, at the same time, should account for all possible outcomes.

Skimming: See *price skimming*.

Slotting Allowance: Incentive payment given to a retailer to allocate shelf space for a new product.

Steal-Share Strategy: Sales-volume-growth strategy aimed at a company's current customers and/or at competitors' customers rather than attracting new category users.

Strategic Business Unit (SBU): An operating company unit with a distinct set of offerings (products and/or services) sold to an identifiable group of customers, in competition with a well-defined set of competitors.

Strategic Group: A set of companies targeting the same customers and following the same strategy.

Sub-Brand: A second-tier brand name often used to mitigate the potential drawbacks of a direct brand extension, while leveraging the core brand to support the extension (e.g., Courtyard by Marriott, Ford Mustang, and Porsche Cayenne).

Supply-Chain Analysis: A method of optimizing the supply side of the manufacturing and/or service delivery process. Supply-chain analysis can be viewed as a subset of the broader concept of *value-chain analysis*.

SWOT Analysis: A popular framework focusing on four aspects of company analysis: strengths, weaknesses, opportunities, and threats (see *SWOT framework*).

Targeting: The process of identifying customers for whom the company and its collaborators can deliver value superior to the competition in a way that allows the company and its collaborators to achieve their strategic goals.

Two-Part Pricing: see *complementary pricing*.

Value-Chain Analysis: A method of optimizing the value-delivery process, from raw materials to the final product.

Vertical Channel Conflict: A conflict that occurs between different levels of the same channel (e.g., manufacturer – retailer) and is often caused by differences in their profit optimization strategies (e.g., the manufacturer prefers that the retailer carry its entire product line, whereas the retailer prefers to carry only the best-selling products from all manufacturers); see also *channel conflict*.

Vertical Extension: An extension is considered vertical if, in addition to being differentiated on non-price benefits, the offering is also differentiated on price (Figure 6). The keyword describing many of the vertical extensions is "better" (which implies price difference in addition to the difference in benefits). Depending on the direction in which the original offering is being extended, two types of vertical extensions can be distinguished: upscale and downscale (see also *extension, horizontal extension*).

Figure 6. Vertical Extension

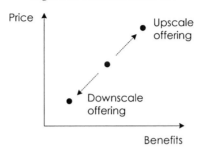

Vertical Integration: The extent to which a firm owns its upstream suppliers and its downstream buyers. Extending ownership upstream (toward suppliers) is referred to as backward integration, while extending ownership of activities downstream (toward buyers) is referred to as forward integration. Some of the common benefits of integration include increased control, reduced costs, optimized channel coordination and profits, and creation of barriers to entry. Some of the common drawbacks include high up-front investment, potential internal inefficiencies due to lack of competition, and capacity sub-optimization resulting from fluctuations in supply and/or demand. Common alternatives to vertical integration include long-term contracts, joint ventures, and franchise agreements.

Volume Discount: Reduction of list price based on the quantity a buyer purchases.

Yield Management Pricing: Pricing strategy whereby price is set to maximize revenue for a set amount of capacity at a given time (typically used by airlines, hotels, etc.)

Notes

[1] Anderson, Erin, et al. (2001), *Marketing Channels* (6th ed.). Upper Saddle River, NJ: Prentice Hall.

[2] Henderson, Bruce, D. (1974), "The Experience Curve Reviewed: Why Does It Work?," in *Perspectives on Strategy: From the Boston Consulting Group* (1998), W.S. Carl and J. George Stalk, Eds. New York, NY: Wiley.

[3] Henderson, Bruce, D. (1973), "The Experience Curve Reviewed: History," in *Perspectives on Strategy: From the Boston Consulting Group* (1998), W.S. Carl and J. George Stalk, Eds. New York, NY: Wiley.

[4] Koch, Richard (1998), *The 80/20 Principle: The Secret to Success by Achieving More with Less.* New York, NY: Doubleday.

[5] Ansoff, H. Igor (1979), *Strategic Management.* New York, NY: Wiley.

Essential Financial Concepts

Break-Even Analysis: Analysis aimed at identifying the break-even point at which the benefits and costs associated with a particular action are equal and beyond which profit occurs. The four most common types of break-even analyses are: (1) *break-even of a fixed-cost investment*, (2) *break-even of a price cut*, (3) *break-even of a variable-cost increase*, and (4) *cannibalization break-even analysis*.

Break-Even Analysis of a Fixed-Cost Investment: Break-even analysis of a fixed-cost investment identifies the sales volume at which a company neither makes a profit nor incurs a loss after making a fixed-cost investment (see Appendix 2 for more details).

Break-Even Analysis of a Price Cut: Break-even analysis of a price cut identifies the increase in the sales volume that needs to be achieved in order for the price cut to have no impact on profitability (see Appendix 3 for more details).

Break-Even Analysis of a Variable-Cost Increase: Break-even analysis of a variable-cost increase identifies the increase in the sales volume that needs to be achieved in order for the increase in variable costs to have no impact on profitability (see Appendix 4 for more details).

Break-Even Analysis of Cannibalization: Break-even analysis of cannibalization identifies the ratio of the cannibalized sales volume of an existing offering to the sales volume generated by a new offering at which a company neither makes a profit nor incurs a loss (see Appendix 5 for more details).

Contribution Margin ($): When expressed in monetary terms ($), contribution margin typically refers to the difference between total revenues and total variable costs. Contribution margin can also be calculated on a per-unit basis as the difference between unit selling price and unit variable cost. Per-unit margin expressed in monetary terms ($) is also referred to as contribution (i.e., the dollar amount that each unit sold "contributes" to the payment of fixed costs).

$$\text{Margin}_{\text{Total}}(\$) = \text{Revenue}_{\text{Total}} - \text{Variable costs}_{\text{Total}}$$

$$\text{Margin}_{\text{Unit}}(\$) = \text{Price}_{\text{Unit}} - \text{Variable costs}_{\text{Unit}}$$

Contribution Margin (%): When expressed in percentages (%), contribution margin typically refers to the ratio of the difference between total revenues and total variable costs to total revenues. Contribution margin also can be expressed as the ratio of unit contribution to unit selling price.

$$\text{Margin (\%)} = \frac{\text{Revenue}_{\text{Total}} - \text{Variable cost}_{\text{Total}}}{\text{Revenue}_{\text{Total}}} = \frac{\text{Price}_{\text{Unit}} - \text{Variable costs}_{\text{Unit}}}{\text{Price}_{\text{Unit}}}$$

Cost of Goods Sold (COGS): Expenses directly related to creating the goods or services being sold. Cost of goods sold can have a *variable* (e.g., the cost of raw materials, the cost of turning raw materials into goods) and a *fixed* component (e.g., depreciation of equipment).

Cross-Elasticity of Demand: The percentage change in quantity sold of a given offering caused by a percentage change in a marketing variable for another offering (e.g., advertising, sales promotions, price).

Cross-Price Elasticity: The percentage change in quantity sold of a given offering caused by a percentage change in the price of another offering.

Fixed Costs: Fixed costs are expenses that do not fluctuate with output volume within a relevant time period (see Appendix 1 for more details).

Goodwill: Accounting term referring to a company's intangible assets. Goodwill is recorded on a company's books when it acquires another company and pays a premium over the listed book value of its assets. The excess paid is categorized as goodwill, added to the acquiring company's balance sheet as an asset, and then depreciated over time (usually 15 years). The Internal Revenue Code defines goodwill as the value of a trade or business attributable to the expectancy of continued customer patronage. Such value results from several factors, including quality product lines and stable employees.

Gross (Profit) Margin: Gross margin is the ratio of *gross profit* to gross revenues (sometimes also used as a synonym for gross profit). Gross margin analysis is a useful tool because it implicitly includes unit-selling prices of products or services, unit costs, and unit volume. Note, however, the difference between *gross margin* and *contribution margin*: Contribution margin includes all variable costs; in contrast, gross margin includes some, but often not all, *variable costs,* a number of which can be part of the *operating margin.*

$$\text{Gross margin} = \frac{\text{Gross profit}}{\text{Gross revenue}} = \frac{\text{Gross revenue - Cost of goods sold}}{\text{Gross revenue}}$$

Gross Profit: Gross profit is the difference between total sales revenue and total cost of goods sold. Gross profit can be also calculated on a per-unit basis as the difference between unit selling price and unit cost of goods sold. To illustrate, if a company sells 100 units, each priced at $1 and each costing the company $.30 to manufacture, then the unit gross profit is $.70, the total gross profit is $70, and the unit and total gross margins are 70%.

$$\text{Gross profit}_{\text{Total}} = \text{Gross revenues}_{\text{Total}} - \text{Cost of goods sold}_{\text{Total}}$$

$$\text{Gross profit}_{\text{Unit}} = \text{Price}_{\text{Unit}} - \text{Cost of goods sold}_{\text{Unit}}$$

Income Statement: Financial document showing a company's income and expenses over a given period (see Appendix 6).

Margin: Margins reflect the difference between two factors and are typically expressed either in monetary terms or percentages. There are two types of margins: (1) contribution margins, which reflect the relationship between variable and fixed costs and (2) income margins, which reflect the relationships between a company's gross profit, income, and gross revenues. See also *gross margin, contribution margin, net margin, operating margin,* and *income statement.*

Marginal Cost: The cost of producing one extra unit.

Market Share: A brand's share of the total sales of all offerings within the product category in which the brand competes. Market share is determined by dividing a brand's sales volume by the total category sales volume, where sales can be defined in terms of revenues or on a unit basis (e.g., number of items sold or number of customers served).

$$\text{Market share} = \frac{\text{An offering's sales in market X}}{\text{Total sales in market X}}$$

Market Size: Monetary value of an existing or potential market, typically on an annual basis. Market size is also used in reference to the number of customers comprising a particular market.

Net Earnings: see *net income.*

Net Income: *Gross revenues* minus all costs and expenses (e.g., cost of goods sold, operating expenses, depreciation, interest, and taxes) in a given period of time.

$$\text{Net income} = \text{Gross revenues - Total costs}$$

Net Margin: Net margin is the ratio of *net income* to gross revenues.

$$\text{Net margin} = \frac{\text{Net income}}{\text{Gross revenues}}$$

Operating Expenses: The primary costs, other than cost of goods sold, incurred in order to generate revenues (e.g., sales, marketing, R&D, general and administrative expenses).

Operating Income: *Gross profit* minus *operating expenses.* Operating income reflects the firm's profitability from current operations without regard for the interest charges accruing from the capital structure.

$$\text{Operating income} = \text{Gross profit - Operating expenses}$$

Operating Margin: Operating margin is the ratio of *operating income* to gross revenues.

$$\text{Operating margin} = \frac{\text{Operating income}}{\text{Gross revenues}}$$

Price Elasticity: A variable representing the percentage change in quantity sold relative to the percentage change in price for a given product or service. Because the quantity demanded decreases when the price increases, this ratio is negative; however, for practical purposes, the absolute value of the ratio is taken, and price elasticity is often reported as a positive number. To illustrate, price elasticity of -2 means that a 5% price increase will result in a 10% decrease in the quantity sold. In cases where price elasticity is greater than one ($|E_p| > 1$), the demand is said to be elastic in the sense that a change in price will cause an even larger change in quantity demanded. In contrast, when price elasticity is less than one ($|E_p| < 1$), the demand is said to be inelastic, meaning that a change in price will result in a smaller change in quantity demanded. When price elasticity is equal to one ($|E_p| = 1$), the demand is said to be unitary, meaning that a change in price will result in an equal change in quantity demanded. Note that because it reflects proportional changes, price elasticity does not depend on the units in which the price and quantity are expressed. Note also that because price elasticity is a function of the initial values, the same absolute changes in price can lead to different price elasticity values. To illustrate, the impact of lowering the price by 5 cents will vary based on the initial price: it is 5% of an initial price of $1.00 but only 1% of an initial price of $5.00.

$$E_p = \frac{\Delta Q\%}{\Delta P\%} = \frac{\Delta Q \cdot P}{\Delta P \cdot Q}$$

Total Costs: The sum of the fixed and variable costs (see Appendix 1 for more details).

Trade Margin: Trade margin is the difference between unit selling price and unit cost at each level of a marketing channel (see Appendix 7). A trade margin is frequently referred to as a markup by channel members and is often expressed as a percentage. Trade margins are typically determined on the basis of selling price, but practices vary among firms and industries.

Variable Costs: Variable costs are expenses that fluctuate in direct proportion to the output volume of units produced (see Appendix 1 for more details).

Variable Profit: The difference between *gross revenues* and *variable costs*.

Exhibit 1: Fixed, Variable, and Total Costs

Cost accounting identifies three basic types of costs: fixed costs, variable costs, and total costs. These three cost types are outlined in more detail below.

Fixed costs are expenses that do not fluctuate with output volume within a relevant time period. Typical examples of fixed costs include research and development expenses, mass-media advertising expenses, rent, interest on debt, insurance, plant and equipment expenses, and salary of permanent full-time workers. Note that even though their absolute size remains unchanged regardless of the output volume, fixed costs become progressively smaller per unit of output as volume increases, a decrease that results from the larger number of output units over which fixed costs are allocated.

In contrast, *variable costs* are expenses that fluctuate in direct proportion to the output volume of units produced. To illustrate, expenses incurred by consumer incentives (e.g., coupons, price discounts, and rebates) are commonly viewed as variable marketing costs. Other expenses such as channel incentives (e.g., promotional allowances) and sales force compensation can be classified either as fixed or variable costs depending on their structure (e.g., performance-based compensation vs. fixed salary).

Finally, the term *total costs* refers to the sum of the fixed and variable costs. The relationship between fixed, variable, and total costs is shown in Figure 1.

Figure 1: The Relationship between Fixed, Variable, and Total Costs

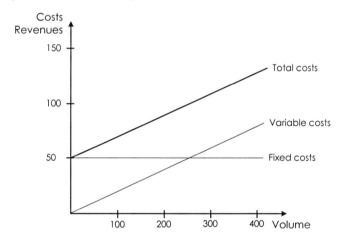

It is important to note that deciding which costs are fixed and which costs are variable depends on the time horizon. To illustrate, in the short run, the salaries of permanent full-time employees will be considered as fixed costs because they do not depend on the output volume. In the longer run, however, a company might adjust the number and/or the salaries of the permanent employees based on the demand for its products or services – a scenario in which these costs would be considered variable rather than fixed. Thus, in the long run, all costs would be considered variable.

Exhibit 2: Break-Even Analysis of a Fixed Cost Investment

Break-even analysis of a fixed-cost investment identifies the unit or dollar sales volume at which the company is able to recoup a particular investment such as research and development expenses, product improvement costs, and/or the costs of an advertising campaign. The break-even volume of a fixed-cost investment (BEV$_{FC}$) is the ratio of the size of the fixed-cost investment to the unit margin.

$$BEV_{FC} = \frac{\text{Fixed-cost investment}}{\text{Unit margin}}$$

Because the unit margin can be expressed as the difference between the unit selling price and unit variable costs, the break-even volume is also often given as:

$$BEV_{FC} = \frac{\text{Fixed-cost investment}}{\text{Unit selling price - Unit variable cost}}$$

The break-even analysis of a fixed cost investment can be illustrated as shown in Figure 2.

Figure 2: Break-Even of a Fixed Cost Investment

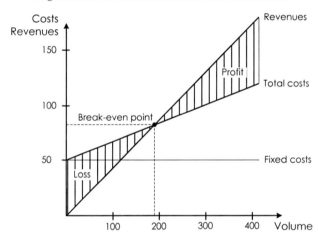

To illustrate, consider an offering priced at $100 with variable costs of $50 and fixed costs of $50M. In this case,

$$BEV_{FC} = \frac{\text{Fixed-cost investment}}{\text{Unit margin}} = \frac{\$50M}{\$100 - \$50} = 1,000,000$$

This implies that in order for the $50M fixed-cost investment to break even, the sales volume should reach 1,000,000 items.

In addition to the break-even analysis of a fixed cost investment associated with launching a new offering, a company might need to calculate the break-even volume of a change (most often an increase) in its current fixed-cost investment. Typical problems to which this type of analysis could be applied are estimating the incremental increase in sales necessary to cover the costs of an R&D project, the costs of an advertising campaign, and even the costs of increasing the compensation package of senior executives. The break-even analysis of such increase in the fixed-cost investment is shown in Figure 3.

Figure 3: Break-Even of an Increase in the Fixed-Cost Investment

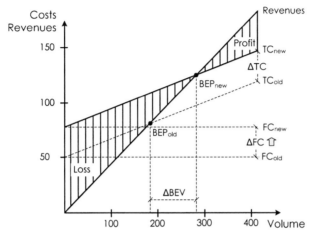

To illustrate, consider the impact of an increase in the fixed costs from $50M to $60M for a product priced at $100 with variable costs of $50. In this case,

$$\text{BEV}_{\Delta FC} = \frac{\text{Increase in the fixed-cost investment}}{\text{Unit margin}} = \frac{\$60M\text{-}\$50M}{\$100\text{-}\$50} = 200,000$$

This implies that in order for the $10M fixed-cost investment to break even, the sales volume should increase by 200,000 items.

Exhibit 3: Break-Even Analysis of a Price Cut

The impact of a price cut on profitability is twofold. On one hand, lowering the price tends to increase the unit volume sold, thus increasing total revenues. On the other hand, lowering the price decreases the unit margin, thus lowering total revenues. In this context, break-even analysis estimates the increase in sales volume that needs to be achieved in order for the price cut to have a neutral impact on profitability. The break-even analysis of a price cut is shown in Figure 4.

Figure 4: Break-Even of a Decrease in Revenues (Due to a Price Cut)

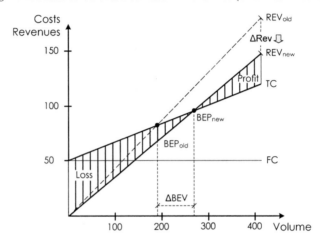

To break even, lost profits resulting from the lower margin due to the price cut must be equal to the additional profits generated from the incremental volume due to low price. Thus, to have a neutral or positive impact on the company's bottom line, the additional profits generated from the incremental volume resulting from the low price must be equal to or greater than the lost profits that result from the lower margin.

$$\text{Profit}_{\text{NewPrice}} \geq \text{Profit}_{\text{OldPrice}} \quad (1)$$

Given that profit is a function of unit volume and unit margin, the above equation can be modified as follows:

$$\text{Volume}_{\text{NewPrice}} \cdot \text{Margin}_{\text{NewPrice}} \geq \text{Volume}_{\text{OldPrice}} \cdot \text{Margin}_{\text{OldPrice}} \quad (2)$$

Now, the above equation can be restructured as follows:

$$\text{Volume}_{\text{NewPrice}} \geq \frac{\text{Margin}_{\text{OldPrice}}}{\text{Margin}_{\text{NewPrice}}} \cdot \text{Volume}_{\text{OldPrice}} \quad (3)$$

Hence, the sales volume that needs to be achieved for a price cut to break even is:

$$\text{BEV}_{\text{PC}} = \frac{\text{Margin}_{\text{OldPrice}}}{\text{Margin}_{\text{NewPrice}}} \cdot \text{Volume}_{\text{OldPrice}} \quad (4)$$

In addition to calculating the break-even volume of a price cut, it might be useful to calculate the rate at which the sales volume must increase in order for the price cut to be profitable. In this context, the break-even rate of a price cut (BER_{PC}) can be derived from equation (2) as follows:

$$\frac{Volume_{NewPrice}}{Volume_{OldPrice}} \geq \frac{Margin_{OldPrice}}{Margin_{NewPrice}} \quad (5)$$

$$\frac{Volume_{NewPrice}}{Volume_{OldPrice}} - 1 \geq \frac{Margin_{OldPrice}}{Margin_{NewPrice}} - 1 \quad (6)$$

$$\frac{Volume_{NewPrice} - Volume_{OldPrice}}{Volume_{OldPrice}} \geq \frac{Margin_{OldPrice}}{Margin_{NewPrice}} - 1 \quad (7)$$

Note that the right side of the equation reflects the increase in volume resulting from the price cut as a percentage of the initial volume before the price cut. Hence, the Break-Even Rate (BER_{PC}) at which sales should increase so that the price cut has neutral impact on profitability is:

$$BER_{PC} = \frac{Margin_{OldPrice}}{Margin_{NewPrice}} - 1 \quad (8)$$

To illustrate, consider the impact of a price cut from \$100 to \$75 for a product with a variable cost of \$50. In this case, $Margin_{OldPrice}$ = \$100 - \$50 = \$50 and $Margin_{NewPrice}$ = \$100 - \$75 = \$25. Therefore, the break-even volume can be calculated as follows:

$$BEV_{PC} = \frac{Margin_{OldPrice}}{Margin_{NewPrice}} \cdot Volume_{OldPrice} = \frac{\$50}{\$25} \cdot Volume_{OldPrice} = 2 \cdot Volume_{OldPrice}$$

This essentially means that in order for the price cut to break even, the sales volume should double at the lower price. It is noteworthy that relatively small changes in the sales price could require what might appear to be a disproportionately greater increase in sales volume. Indeed, in the example above, a 25% decrease in price requires doubling the sales volume.

Alternatively, one could calculate the rate at which the current volume should increase so that the price cut has neutral impact on profitability.

$$BER_{PC} = \frac{Margin_{OldPrice}}{Margin_{NewPrice}} - 1 = \frac{\$50}{\$25} - 1 = 1$$

The above calculation means that in order for the price cut to break even, the sales volume should increase by a factor of 1, or by 100%.

Exhibit 4: Break-Even Analysis of a Variable-Cost Increase

Break-even analysis of a variable-cost increase identifies the sales volume at which a company neither makes a profit nor incurs a loss after increasing the variable costs associated with a particular offering. Typical problems to which this type of analysis can be applied are estimating the incremental increase in sales necessary to cover an increase in the cost of goods sold, estimating the costs associated with increasing the item-specific level of service, and estimating the costs associated with running item-specific incentives (e.g., premiums). The break-even analysis of a variable-cost increase is shown in Figure 5.

Figure 5: Break-Even of a Variable-Cost Increase

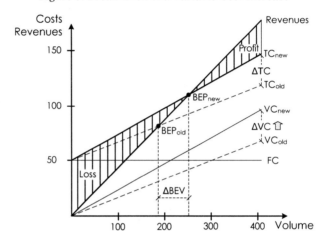

The basic principle of calculating the break-even point of an increase in an offering's variable costs is similar to that of estimating the break-even point of a price cut. The key difference in this case is that the decrease in the margin generated by the new offering is a result of an increase in the offering's costs rather than a decrease in revenues. Thus, the break-even volume of a variable-cost increase can be calculated as follows:

$$BEV_{VC} = \frac{Margin_{OldVC}}{Margin_{NewVC}} \cdot Volume_{OldVC}$$

Similarly, the break-even rate of an increase in the variable costs can be calculated as follows:

$$BER_{VC} = \frac{Margin_{OldVC}}{Margin_{NewVC}} - 1$$

To illustrate, consider the impact of an increase in variable costs from $50 to $60 for a product priced at $100. In this case, $Margin_{OldVC}$ = $100 - $50 = $50 and $Margin_{NewVC}$ = $100 - $60 = $40. Therefore, the break-even volume of a variable-cost increase can be calculated as follows:

$$BEV_{VC} = \frac{Margin_{OldVC}}{Margin_{NewVC}} \cdot Volume_{OldVC} = \frac{\$50}{\$40} \cdot Volume_{OldVC} = 1.25 \cdot Volume_{OldVC}$$

This means that in order for the variable-cost increase to break even, the sales volume should increase by a factor of 1.25 or by 125%.

Alternatively, one could calculate the rate at which the current volume should increase so that the increase in variable costs has neutral impact on profitability.

$$BER_{VC} = \frac{Margin_{OldVC}}{Margin_{NewVC}} - 1 = \frac{\$50}{\$40} - 1 = 0.25$$

The above calculation implies that in order for the increase in variable costs to break even, the sales volume should increase by a factor of .25, or by 25%.

Exhibit 5: Break-Even Analysis of Cannibalization

The primary goal of extending a company's product line by launching a new offering is to increase the company's sales revenues by growing demand for the overall category and/or by stealing share from competitors. A typical side effect of such product line extensions is that, in addition to stealing share from competitors, the new offering also takes away share from a company's current offerings – a process commonly referred to as cannibalization (Figure 6).

Figure 6: The impact of a price cut on sales volume

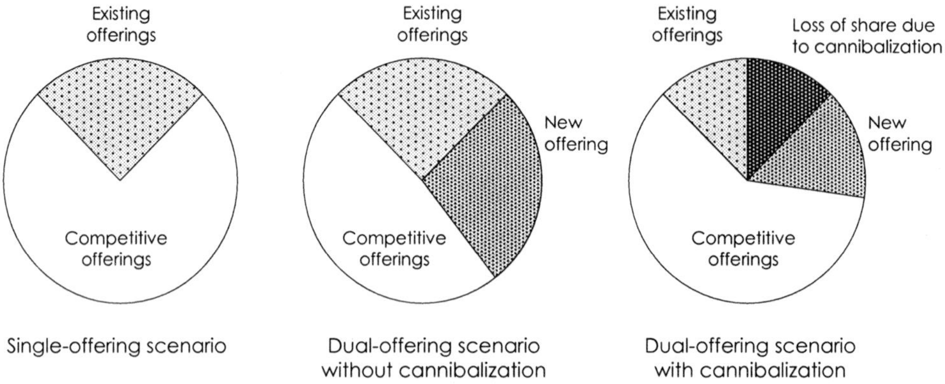

Single-offering scenario

Dual-offering scenario without cannibalization

Dual-offering scenario with cannibalization

In this context, the break-even rate of a potential cannibalization of sales of an existing offering from a product line extension identifies the ratio of the cannibalized sales volume of the existing offering to the sales volume generated by the new offering at which a company neither makes a profit nor incurs a loss. Thus, the break-even rate of cannibalization indicates the maximum proportion of the sales volume of the new offering that could come from the company's existing offering(s) without incurring a loss. The break-even rate of cannibalization can be derived as follows:

To avoid loss of profit across all offerings, the profit from the new product must be equal to or greater than the lost profits from cannibalization (the dark-shaded area in the above chart).

$$\text{Profit}_{\text{NewOffering}} \geq \text{LostProfit}_{\text{OldOffering}} \quad (1)$$

Given that profit is a function of unit volume and unit margin, the above equation can be modified as follows:

$$\text{Volume}_{\text{NewOffering}} \cdot \text{Margin}_{\text{NewOffering}} \geq \text{LostVolume}_{\text{OldOffering}} \cdot \text{Margin}_{\text{OldOffering}} \quad (2)$$

Now, equation (2) can be restructured as follows:

$$\frac{\text{LostVolume}_{\text{OldOffering}}}{\text{Volume}_{\text{NewOffering}}} = \frac{\text{Margin}_{\text{NewOffering}}}{\text{Margin}_{\text{OldOffering}}} \quad (3)$$

Note that the left part of the equation is the ratio of the sales volume of the old offering that was lost due to cannibalization of the sales volume of the new offering – which is exactly the definition of the break-even rate of cannibalization (BER$_C$). Hence,

$$BER_C = \frac{Margin_{NewOffering}}{Margin_{OldOffering}}$$

To illustrate, consider a company launching a new product priced at $70 with variable costs of $60, which might cannibalize the sales of an existing product that is priced at $100 and also has variable costs of $60. In this case, $Margin_{NewOffering}$ = $70 - $60 = $10 and $Margin_{OldOffering}$ = $100 - $60 = $40. Therefore, the break-even rate of cannibalization can be calculated as follows:

$$BER_C = \frac{Margin_{NewOffering}}{Margin_{OldOffering}} = \frac{\$10}{\$40} = 0.25$$

The break-even rate of cannibalization in this case is 0.25 or 25%, which means that in order to be profitable to the company no more than 25% of the sales volume of the new offering should come from the current offering, which in turn implies that at least 75% of sales volume should come from the competitive offering.

Exhibit 6: Income Statement: An Overview

Income statement is a financial document showing a company's income and expenses over a given period. It typically identifies revenues, costs, operating expenses, operating income, and earnings (Figure 7).

Figure 7: An Example of Revenues, Costs, and Margins as Shown in a Company's Income Statement

Gross Revenues	
Product sales	$ 12,000
Services	3,000
Total (Gross) Revenues	15,000
Cost of Goods Sold	
Product costs	4,000
Services costs	1,500
Depreciation	500
Total Cost of Goods Sold	6,000
Gross Profit	9,000
Gross Margin	60%
Operating Expenses	
Sales and Marketing	5,000
General and Administrative	1,000
Research and Development	1,500
Total Operating Expenses	7,500
Operating Income	1,500
Operating Margin	10%
Interest payments on loans	500
Earnings before taxes	1,000
Provision for taxes	250
Net Income (Earnings)	750
Net (Profit) Margin	5%

Exhibit 7: Distribution Channel Margin Analysis

A useful approach to analyzing margins of the individual members of a distribution channel involves mapping the channel structure to identify margins for each channel member (Figure 8).

Figure 8: An Example of Distribution Channel Margins

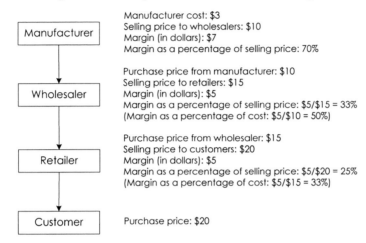

Manufacturer
Manufacturer cost: $3
Selling price to wholesalers: $10
Margin (in dollars): $7
Margin as a percentage of selling price: 70%
Wholesaler
Purchase price from manufacturer: $10
Selling price to retailers: $15
Margin (in dollars): $5
Margin as a percentage of selling price: $5/$15 = 33%
(Margin as a percentage of cost: $5/$10 = 50%)
Retailer
Purchase price from wholesaler: $15
Selling price to customers: $20
Margin (in dollars): $5
Margin as a percentage of selling price: $5/$20 = 25%
(Margin as a percentage of cost: $5/$15 = 33%)
Customer
Purchase price: $20

Note that margins are almost universally calculated based on the sales revenue (e.g., sales price) rather than based on the cost (e.g., purchase price). To illustrate, the margin for an item purchased for $10 (cost) and sold for $15 (revenue) can be calculated as follows:

$$\text{Margin} = \frac{\text{Revenue - Cost}}{\text{Revenue}} = \frac{\text{Selling price - Purchase price}}{\text{Selling price}} = \frac{\$15 - \$10}{\$15} = 0.33$$

Appendix C
Case Analysis Frameworks

This book introduced a number of frameworks that represent some of the most useful approaches to analyzing and solving strategic problems. These frameworks, as well as several other popular frameworks commonly used in case analysis, are briefly summarized below and are outlined in more detail in the following sections.

- **5-C Framework**
  The 5-C framework (customers, company, collaborators, competitors, and context) offers a systematic approach to evaluating the market environment.

- **3-C Framework**
  The 3-C framework (customers, company, and competitors) is a simplified version of the more comprehensive 5-C framework used to evaluate the market environment.

- **C-C-D Value-Management Framework**
  The C-C-D value-management framework (creating value, communicating value, delivering value) is an essential method for designing and evaluating the tactical aspects of an offering.

- **4-P Framework**
  The 4-P framework (product, price, promotion, and place) is a simplified version of the more comprehensive C-C-D framework used to analyze the tactical aspect of an offering.

- **Product-Market Growth Framework**
  The product-market growth framework (also referred to as the Ansoff matrix) is a method for evaluating a company's expansion prospects and for developing sales-growth strategies.

- **SWOT Framework**
  The SWOT framework uses a systematic approach to analyzing a company's overall business condition by evaluating its strengths, weaknesses, opportunities, and threats.

- **The Five Forces Framework**
  The five forces framework is a method for conducting industry analysis, making decisions concerning entering and exiting an industry, and evaluating the competitive aspects of a company's offering.

- **Value-Chain Framework**
  The value-chain framework (supplier, manufacturer, channel, customer) is a systematic approach to examining a company's value-delivery process.

▫ **7-S Framework**
The 7-S framework offers a systematic approach to analyzing the effectiveness of an organization by evaluating its seven key characteristics: strategy, skills, shared values, structure, staff, systems, and style.

▫ **BCG Product-Portfolio Framework**
The BCG product-portfolio framework (also referred to as the BCG matrix) is a method for evaluating the overall performance of a company's strategic business units and for making cash-allocation recommendations.

5-C Framework

Snapshot: Customer, company, collaborators, competitors, context

Overview: Market structure analysis examines how the environment influences an offering's performance in the marketplace. In particular, market structure analysis examines the following five factors, often referred to as the five Cs: (1) customers, (2) the company, (3) collaborators working with the company to deliver the offering to customers, (4) competitors with offerings that provide similar benefits to the same customers, and (5) context (e.g., economic, legal, technological, social, and political) in which the company delivers its offering to customers (Figure 1).

Figure 1. The 5-C Framework for Market Structure Analysis

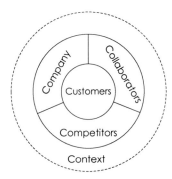

The five factors describing the marketing environment can be summarized as follows.

- *Customer analysis* aims to identify the customers for whom the company's offering can deliver superior value in a way that allows the company and its collaborators to achieve their strategic goals. Identifying target customers involves two decisions: (1) identifying the relevant customer *needs* to be fulfilled by the company's offering and (2) identifying actionable strategies to *reach* customers with these needs (e.g., demographic, geographic, psychographic, and behavioral characteristics that enable the company to communicate and deliver the offering to these customers in an effective and cost-efficient manner).

- *Company analysis* involves identifying distinct capabilities that are critical to achieving a sustainable competitive advantage and, hence, to the company's long-term success in the marketplace. It typically involves evaluating the strategic assets and core competencies that allow the company to satisfy customer needs better than the competition in a way that enables the company and its collaborators to achieve their strategic goals.

- *Collaborator analysis* involves identifying business entities that work with the company to deliver the offering to target customers. In this context, collaboration might involve any of the following areas: product, service, brand, price, incentives, communications, and distribution. To illustrate, companies can collaborate to develop a product (research-and-development collaboration); to deliver the offering to the customer (channel collaboration); and/or to create a customer incentive (promotional collaboration).

o *Competitive analysis* involves identifying business entities with offerings positioned to deliver value to the same customers. Because competitors are defined relative to the needs of the target segment, the competition often goes beyond industry-defined product categories. To illustrate, Kodak competes not only in the 35mm film market with companies like Fuji and Agfa, but also with manufacturers of digital cameras, such as Sony and Canon, and even with the manufacturers of camera-equipped mobile phones, such as Nokia and Ericsson. In this context, 35mm film, digital cameras, and camera-equipped phones are not just substitute products but rather cross-category competitors because they compete to satisfy the same need of the same target customers.

o *Context analysis* involves evaluating factors that describe the relevant aspects of the environment in which the company delivers its offering to customers. Typical context factors include the economic, legal/regulatory, political, and technological environment in which the marketing exchange takes place. To illustrate, the demand for hands-free devices is affected by the legislation requiring hands-free mobile phone use while driving in many cities.

An important characteristic of the 5-C Framework is its visual representation, which reflects the nature of the relationships between the key market factors and the fact that the marketplace is defined by a specific customer need, relative to which the company's collaborators and competitors are defined.

Application: By identifying the key factors that define the environment in which an offering operates, the 5-C framework offers a simple yet comprehensive approach to understanding the marketplace.

3-C Framework

Snapshot: Company, competition, customer

Overview: The 3-C model, advanced by Kenichi Ohmae, suggests that a strategist should focus on three key factors for success: (1) the corporation, (2) the customer, and (3) the competition.[1] By understanding these three factors and integrating them into a strategic framework (or, to use Ohmae's terminology, a strategic triangle), the company can achieve a sustainable competitive advantage.

The corporation's goal is to deliver superior value to its customers, relative to the competition, which, according to Ohmae, results from the corporation's competitive cost advantage. The 3-C framework suggests that managers need to evaluate the business environment in which they operate: the strengths and weaknesses of their own company, the needs of their customers, and the strengths and weaknesses of their competitors. The 3-C framework is simple, intuitive, and easy to understand and use – factors that have contributed to its popularity.

Common Misconceptions: One of the most common misinterpretations of the 3-C framework occurs when unrelated factors also starting with "c," such as capacity and cost,[2] are included as a part of the 3-C model. Recall that the Cs describe the main players in the marketplace (i.e., company, customers, and competitors). Capacity and cost, on the other hand, are characteristics of the company and are not participants in the marketing exchange. Note that the issue here is not whether cost and capacity are important factors in marketing analysis but whether they conform to the logic used to identify the Cs as the main factors that need to be taken into account when designing a company's business strategy. The same logic applies to other potential Cs such as category, complexity, core competencies, and creativity.

Limitations: An important limitation of the 3-C framework is that it does not explicitly account for a number of important environmental factors. To illustrate, a company's collaborators are not part of the 3-C model, despite the important role collaborators (e.g., suppliers and distributors) play in developing and delivering a company's offerings. Another limitation of the 3-C framework is that it does not explicitly account for the variety of economic, regulatory, technological, and political factors that comprise the context in which the company operates.

Application: The 3-C framework offers a simple approach for categorizing different aspects of the marketing environment and introduces a simple structure for evaluating various business problems. However, because it excludes important market and environmental factors (i.e., collaborator and context), business analysis can be better served by the more comprehensive 5-C framework discussed earlier.

C-C-D Value Management Framework

Snapshot: Creating, communicating, and delivering value

Overview: The C-C-D framework identifies how the desired strategy is implemented through a set of specific marketing actions aimed at creating, communicating, and delivering value. Value creation captures the attributes and processes that define the value of the offering to customers, the company, and its collaborators. Value communication encompasses the attributes and processes that create awareness of the offering among target customers, within the company, and to collaborators. Finally, value delivery involves transfer of the offering value to customers, the company, and its collaborators.

Creating, communicating, and delivering value is implemented through a set of specific marketing activities commonly referred to as the marketing mix. In particular, seven key marketing mix variables can be identified: product, service, brand, price, incentives, communication, and distribution. These seven marketing mix variables can be related to the three aspects of the value management process, as shown in Figure 2. Here, the product, service, brand, price, and incentives comprise the value-creation aspect of the offering; communications capture the communication aspect; and distribution reflects the delivery aspect of the value management process.

Figure 2. The C-C-D Value Management Framework

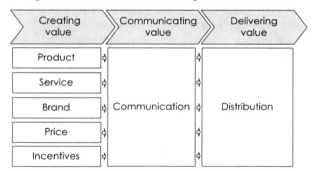

The three key aspects of the value-management process – creating, communicating, and delivering value – can be summarized as follows:

o   The value-creation process is typically carried out through a combination of five marketing mix variables: product, service, brand, price, and incentives. The key aspects of these marketing mix variables are outlined in more detail below:

-   The *product* and *service* components of the marketing mix reflect the functional characteristics of the offering. The key differences between the product and service aspect of an offering concern the change of ownership and separability. Thus, unlike products that typically change ownership in the process of the marketing exchange, services do not necessarily imply a change in ownership. In addition, unlike products that could be physically and/or temporally separated from the manufacturer, services are typically delivered and consumed at the same time, which implies that they typically cannot be inventoried or distributed through multiple distribution channels.

- The *brand* component of the marketing mix captures the characteristics of the offering typically associated with its identity and is usually the main source of the offering's psychological value. In this context, the key functions of the brand are to identify a company and/or a company's offering, to differentiate it from the competition, and to create value for customers, the company, and its collaborators. Commonly used brand elements include brand name, logo, symbol, character, and slogan.

- The *price* reflects the monetary aspect of the benefits delivered by the offering. Commonly used benchmarks for price setting are: company factors (e.g., company goals, cost structure); collaborator factors (e.g., collaborator goals, cost structure); competitive tactics (e.g., competitive prices, cost structure); and customer demand function (e.g., customers' willingness to pay). An optimal pricing strategy will typically take into account all four factors to set the optimal value for customers, the company, and its collaborators.

- *Incentives* enhance the value of the offering by providing additional benefits and/or reducing costs. These are usually short-term solutions aimed at increasing the sales volume of the offering. Monetary incentives typically include activities such as trade allowances, volume discounts, price reductions, coupons, and rebates. Non-monetary incentives include samples, premiums, and rewards. As in the case of the other marketing mix variables, incentives need to be optimized with respect to their value to customers, the company, and its collaborators.

o The *communications component* of the marketing mix aims to promote the offering by informing the target audience about the offering as a whole or highlighting its particular characteristics: product, service, brand, price, and incentives. The most popular means of communication is advertising in all of its forms (e.g., television, radio, print, online, outdoor, point-of-purchase, event sponsorship, and product placement). Other forms of communication include public relations aimed at generating publicity about the offering, and personal selling.

o The distribution component of the marketing mix captures the channel structure through which the offering is delivered to customers, the company, and its collaborators. The different aspects of value delivery include delivery of the product, service, brand, price, and incentive components of the offering. The value-delivery channels can be classified into three basic types: direct channels, in which the company delivers its offering directly to recipients without relying on intermediaries; indirect channels, which typically involve one or more intermediaries (e.g., distributors, wholesalers, and/or retailers); and hybrid channels, which involve a combination of direct and indirect channels.

Application: A replacement for the outdated 4-P model, the C-C-D value-management framework is an essential method for designing and evaluating the tactical aspects of an offering.

4-P Framework

Snapshot: Product, price, promotion, place

Overview: The 4-P model, introduced by Jerome McCarthy, offers a tool for planning and analyzing the implementation of a given marketing strategy.[3] According to this model, there are four key decisions that managers must make with respect to a given offering: what features to include in the product, how to price the product, how to promote the product, and in which distribution channels to "place" the product. These four decisions, often referred to as the marketing mix, are captured by the four P's: product, price, promotion, and place.

Common Misconceptions: Most misinterpretations of the 4-P framework arise when managers try to fit different factors into the framework and focus on finding a factor starting with "p" rather than on the underlying logic. To illustrate, a common misinterpretation of the four Ps involves adding positioning, people, or personnel as one of the Ps. Positioning is not a marketing mix variable; rather, it is part of a company's overall strategy, which is then implemented through a particular combination of the marketing mix variables. In the same vein, people and personnel are typically viewed as an integral part of the company, rather than as a part of an offering's marketing mix. Another common misinterpretation of the 4-P framework concerns the use of "placement" instead of "place." Note that the term "placement" is commonly used in reference to a promotional strategy that involves embedding a product in various forms of entertainment.

Limitations: The first and most obvious limitation is the absence of separate service and image (brand) components in the 4-P model. Indeed, because it was developed to explain the process involved in marketing consumer-packaged goods, the 4-P model does not explicitly account for the service element of the offering – a key drawback in today's service-oriented business environment. Furthermore, the 4-P model does not explicitly consider the brand as a separate marketing mix variable. Instead, the brand is viewed as a part of a company's product and/or promotion decisions.

Another potential problem concerns the term "promotion." Promotion is a very broad term that includes two distinct types of marketing variables: incentives (e.g., price promotions, coupons, dealer incentives) and communications (e.g., advertising, public relations). While it is a common accounting practice to combine these factors, they each have a distinct impact on business processes; hence, for the purposes of strategic analysis, they should be considered independently from one another.

Finally, the use of the term "place" as an element of the marketing mix can be questioned, as well. As the process of delivering the company's offering to customers becomes increasingly complex, it is more accurate to refer to this process as "distribution" or "channel" rather than simply as "place." In fact, the term "place" is rarely used in business analysis.

Reconceptualization: Despite its limitations, the basic concept underlying the 4-P framework is logical and can be interpreted in the context of the strategic marketing framework outlined earlier in this book. In this context, the product and the price represent the processes of creating value; promotions represent the value-creation (incentive) and communication aspects of the offering; and the place represents the value-delivery aspect of the offering (Figure 3).

Figure 3. Re-conceptualizing the 4-P Framework

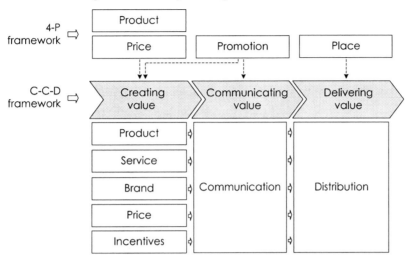

Application: The 4-P framework offers an overview of the key decision variables involved in the implementation of a given marketing strategy. Because of its limitations, however, business analysis can be better served by a more comprehensive and up-to-date C-C-D framework discussed earlier.

Product-Market Growth Framework

Snapshot: A 2 x 2 matrix identifying four common market-growth strategies: market penetration, market development, product development, and diversification

Overview: The product-market growth matrix, introduced by Igor Ansoff,[4] is a 2 x 2 matrix in which one of the factors is given by the type of offering (existing vs. new) and the other factor by the type of customers (current vs. new). The resulting four product-market strategies are commonly referred to as (1) market penetration, (2) market development, (3) product development, and (4) diversification (Figure 4).

Figure 4. Product-Market Growth Matrix[5]

	Current Customers	New Customers
Current Products	Market penetration	Market development
New Products	Product development	Diversification

The four product-market growth strategies can be summarized as follows:

o   *Market-penetration* strategies aim to increase the sales of an existing offering to a company's current customers. A common market-penetration strategy is increasing the usage rate. To illustrate, airlines stimulate the demand from current customers by adopting frequent-flyer programs; packaged goods manufacturers enclose re-purchase coupons as part of their product offerings; orange juice manufacturers promote drinking orange juice throughout the day rather than for breakfast only.

o   *Market-development* strategies aim to grow sales by introducing an existing offering to new customers. In this case, the company builds on the success of its offerings to attract new customers. The two most common market-development strategies include targeting a new customer segment in an existing geographic area and introducing the offering to a different geographic area (e.g., exporting products to a new country). Market-development strategies aimed at attracting new customers include price promotions (e.g., price reductions, coupons, and rebates), new distribution channels, and communication strategies focused on different customer segment(s).

o   *Product-development* strategies target sales growth by developing new (to the company) offerings for existing customers. In this case, the company builds on its current customer base by offering new products. The two most common market-development strategies include developing entirely new offerings (product innovation) or extending the current product line by modifying existing offerings (product line extension). In this context, product line extensions are often achieved by adding different sizes, forms, flavors, colors, while preserving the core set of benefits of the original offering.

o *Diversification strategies* aim to grow sales by introducing new offerings to new customers. Because both the offering and the customers are new to the company, this strategy is riskier than any of the other product-market strategies. The primary rationale for diversification is to take advantage of growth opportunities in areas in which the company has no presence.

Application: The product-market growth framework is a relatively simple and very useful approach for evaluating a company's expansion options and developing sales growth strategies.

SWOT Framework

Snapshot: Strengths, weaknesses, opportunities, threats

Overview: SWOT analysis is typically used to evaluate the overall health of a particular company. The SWOT framework calls for compartmentalizing all factors describing the company, and the environment in which it operates, into four categories: strengths, weaknesses, opportunities, and threats. These factors can be viewed on two dimensions: (1) whether they are internal or external to the company, and (2) whether they are favorable or unfavorable from the company's standpoint. The resulting 2 x 2 SWOT matrix is shown in Figure 5.

Figure 5. SWOT Matrix

	Favorable Factors	Unfavorable Factors
Internal Factors	Strengths	Weaknesses
External Factors	Opportunities	Threats

To illustrate, factors such as loyal customers, strong brand name(s), strategically important patents and trademarks, know-how, experienced personnel, and access to scarce resources would be classified as strengths; whereas, factors such as disloyal customers, diluted brand name, and lack of technological expertise would be classified as weaknesses. Similarly, factors such as emergence of a new, underserved customer segment, low price-sensitivity customers, and a favorable economic environment would be classified as opportunities. In contrast, factors such as a new competitive entry into the category, increased product commoditization, and increased buyer and/or supplier power would be classified as threats.

Application: The SWOT framework is a relatively simple, extremely flexible, and very intuitive approach for evaluating a company's overall business condition.

The Five Forces Framework

Snapshot: Bargaining power of suppliers, bargaining power of buyers, threat of new entrants, threat of substitutes, and rivalry among extant competitors.

Overview: The five forces framework was advanced by Michael Porter[6] as a conceptual approach for industry-based analysis of the nature of the competition.

According to the Five Forces framework, the competitiveness within an industry is determined by evaluating the following five factors: bargaining power of suppliers, bargaining power of buyers, threat of new entrants, threat of substitutes, and rivalry among extant competitors (Figure 6). The joint impact of these five factors determines the competitive environment in which a firm operates and allows the firm to anticipate competitors' actions.

Figure 6. The Five Forces of Competition[7]

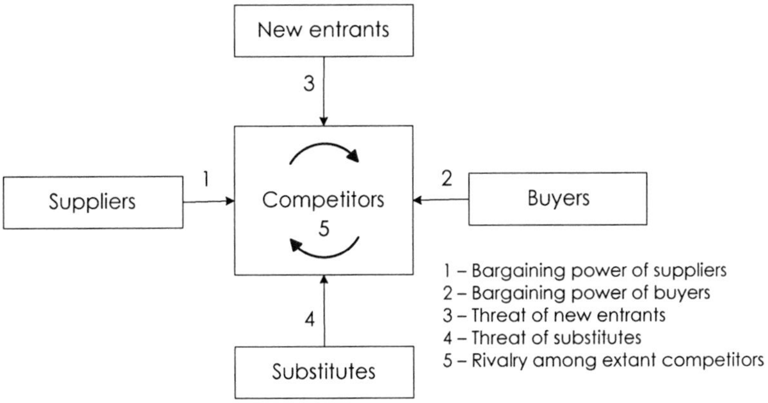

The five forces influencing the state of competition in an industry can be summarized as follows:

Bargaining power of suppliers. A supplier group is powerful when it is dominated by a few companies; the product is differentiated and/or has switching costs; the product has diverse applications (e.g., across industries); the product poses a credible threat of forward integration.

Bargaining power of buyers. A buyer group is powerful when it has concentrated large-volume purchases; the supplied product is undifferentiated and has no switching costs; the product represents a substantial part of buyers' costs (hence encouraging more price shopping); the buyer's profit margins are low; the product is not crucial for the buyer; there is a credible threat of backward integration.

Threat of new entrants. The greater the threat, the greater the overall industry competitiveness. Six main entry barriers can be identified:

   o Economies of scale, which refers to the benefits from operating the business on a large scale (e.g., in terms of production, research, marketing, service, distribution, or utilization of the sales force and financing). As a general rule, economies of scale tend to deter new entrants.

- Product differentiation, which reflects the degree to which competitive products are perceived by consumers to be different. In general, the presence of highly differentiated products is viewed as a deterrent for new entrants.

- Capital requirements, which refer to the magnitude of financial resources required to enter the industry. High capital requirements are likely to deter new entrants.

- Cost disadvantages (independent of size), which capture factors such as experience curve effects, government subsidies, or favorable locations.

- Access to distribution channels, which requires new entrants to find a way to push established companies "off the shelves" in order to sell their product. In this context, limited access to distribution channels tends to serve as a deterrent for new entrants.

- Government policy, which refers to factors such as government regulations, license requirements, and access to technologies (e.g., airlines, power generation, and liquor).

Threat of substitute products or services. The introduction of new products tends to increase the competition in an industry and limit the profitability of an industry. In general, the threat of substitutes tends to be greater in cases when the substitutes have clear advantages over the existing products and/or when the profit margins in the industry producing the substitute product are relatively high.

Rivalry among existing competitors. Rivalry tends to be stronger in cases where existing competitors are numerous and comparable in size and power (and hence are likely to have similar goals); industry growth is slow (leading to fights for redistribution of the existing market share); the product is non-differentiated (leading to price-based competition); the fixed costs are high and/or the product is perishable; there is an excess capacity; the exit barriers are high; rivals are very diverse in terms of goals, strategies, and/or organizational culture.

Application: The five forces is a very popular framework for analyzing the competition within an industry. It is often used for strategic industry-level decisions such as evaluating the viability of entering (or exiting from) a particular industry.

Value-Chain Framework

Snapshot: A systematic approach to examining the value delivery process

Overview: Value-chain analysis uses a descriptive approach to identify a sequence of functional elements in the process of value creation. Based on the level of generality and the underlying assumptions, there are different approaches to value-chain analysis.

A general approach to analyzing the value-chain delivery process involves examining the value added by each member along the supply and distribution chains, as shown in Figure 7. The goal of this analysis is to optimize value creation by maximizing benefits while minimizing costs for each of the channel members.

Figure 7. The Value-Delivery Process: The Big Picture

In addition to analyzing the value delivery process across different value-chain members (e.g., supplier, manufacturer, wholesaler, and retailer), value-chain analysis can be applied to examine the value-creation processes within each member of the value chain. A relatively simple framework for company-focused value-chain analysis involves a model with three main components: inputs, processes, and outputs (Figure 8). The inputs are factors such as the inbound logistics and raw materials/labor used in developing the company's offering; processes are the value-creating activities that transform the inputs into the end product; and outputs capture factors such as the outbound logistics and the value added after the product leaves the company.

Figure 8. The Value-Delivery Model: A Company Perspective

Another popular approach to company-focused value-chain analysis is the one introduced by Michael Porter.[8] It distinguishes between two types of activities: primary activities and support activities (Figure 9). Primary activities are directly concerned with the creation or delivery of a product or service. They can be grouped into five main areas: inbound logistics (includes receiving, storing, inventory control, transportation scheduling); operations (machining, packaging, assembly, equipment maintenance, testing, and all other value-creating activities that transform the inputs into the final product); outbound logistics (activities required to get the finished product to customers, such as warehousing, order fulfillment, transportation, distribution management); marketing and sales (activities associated with getting buyers to purchase the product, including channel selection, advertising, promotion, selling, pricing, and retail management); and service (activities that maintain and enhance the product's value, including customer support, repair services, installation, training, spare parts management, and upgrading).

Figure 9. The Value-Delivery Analysis: A Company Perspective[9]

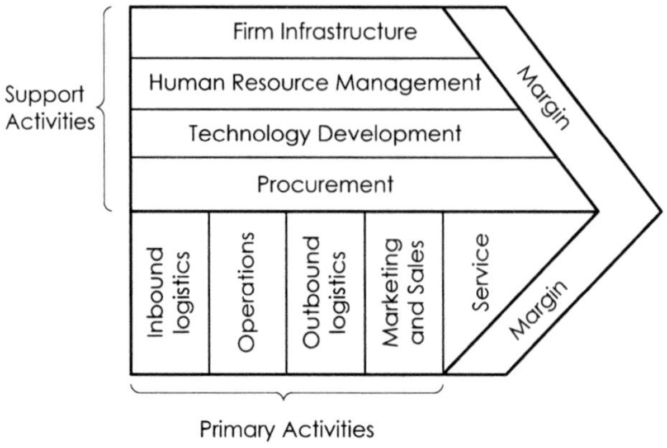

Each of these primary activities is linked to support activities that help improve their effectiveness or efficiency. There are four main areas of support activities: procurement (raw materials, servicing, spare parts, buildings, and machines); technology development (e.g., research and development, process automation, and design); human resource management (e.g., recruiting, development, retention and compensation of employees and managers); and infrastructure (e.g., general management, planning management, legal, finance, accounting, and quality management).

Application: The value-chain analysis is a useful tool for understanding the nature of the value-delivery process and optimizing the process by removing potential inefficiencies.

7-S Framework

Snapshot: Strategy, skills, shared values, structure, staff, systems, style

Overview: The basic idea of identifying several core factors to evaluate the effectiveness of an organization first appeared in *The Art of Japanese Management*[10] and was later introduced as the McKinsey 7-S Framework in Peters and Waterman's bestseller *In Search of Excellence*.[11] The 7-S framework involves analyzing seven interdependent aspects of a firm: strategy; skills (institutional capabilities such as the distinctive capabilities of personnel); shared values (culture – what the organization stands for and its central beliefs); structure (organization – the way the company's units relate to one another); staff (people – types of personnel within the organization, management training); systems (procedures – financial systems, information systems, as well as hiring, promotion and performance appraisal systems); and style (leadership style – how key managers work toward achieving the organization's goals). Working synergistically, these key factors account for the effectiveness of an organization. In this context, the 7-S framework calls for evaluating the seven key organizational factors and analyzing the relationships among them to ensure consistency (Figure 10).

Figure 10. 7-S Framework[12]

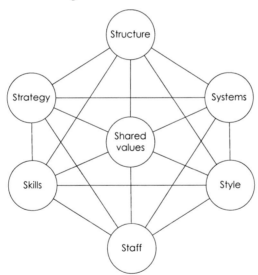

Application: McKinsey's 7-S framework is a very useful approach for analyzing the internal effectiveness and efficiency of an organization.

BCG Product-Portfolio Framework

Snapshot: A 2 x 2 matrix for classifying and managing a company's strategic business units – stars (hold), question marks (build), cash cow (harvest), dogs (divest)

Overview: The BCG product-portfolio model is based on the notion that to be successful a company should have a portfolio of products with different market shares and different growth rates. The portfolio composition is viewed as a function of balancing cash flows between high-growth and low-growth products. In this context, the main goal of the BCG product portfolio model is to guide the cash-allocation decisions across different strategic business units (SBUs) of a company.

The BCG model is based on two key assumptions. The first assumption is that profit margins are a function of market share, such that high market share leads to high margins. This assumption is derived from the experience curve effect and, in particular, from the notion that increasing the scale of production leads to a lower cost structure and, hence, to higher profit margins.[13] The second assumption is that profit margins are a function of the growth of the industry in which the company operates and that different stages of growth require different cash-management strategies. In particular, high-growth businesses require cash investment, whereas low-growth businesses tend to generate cash in excess of what needs to be reinvested to maintain share. These two assumptions are reflected in the fact that market share and market growth are the two key components of evaluating the performance of a given strategic business unit.

Using the BCG matrix entails two major steps: classification and action. The *classification phase* calls for categorizing all SBUs into four types: question marks, stars, cash cows, and dogs. This categorization is based on each SBU's performance on two factors: (1) relative market share (share relative to the largest competitor) and (2) market growth. Thus, a relative market share of 0.4 means that the SBU has 40% of the market leader's share, and a relative market share of 2.0 means that the SBU is the leader and has twice the share of the next largest competitor (Figure 11). For presentation purposes, the relative market share is drawn on a logarithmic scale. Market growth rate is drawn on a normal scale, with 10% annual market growth often used as the reference point.

Figure 11. BCG Matrix Step 1 (classification)[14]

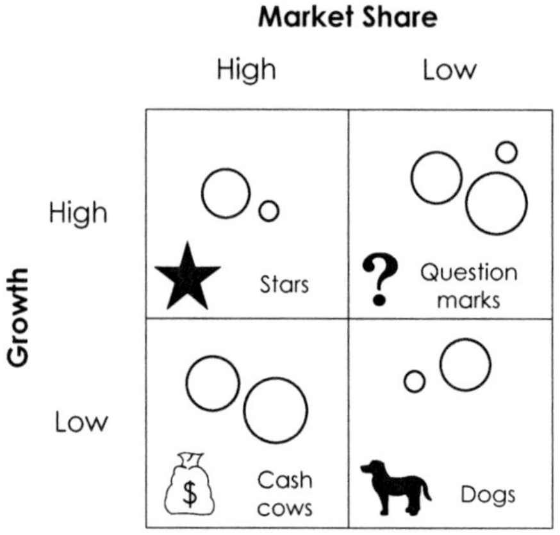

The *action phase* identifies the role to be assigned to each SBU (Figure 12). There are four basic strategies to achieve an efficient resource allocation: (1) Hold (preserve market share, usually applied to "stars"); (2) Build (increase market share and forgo near-term earnings, usually applied to "question marks"); (3) Harvest (increase cash flow and forgo building market share, usually applied to "cash cows"); and (4) Divest (sell or liquidate, usually applied to "dogs").

Figure 12. BCG Matrix: Step 2 (action)[15]

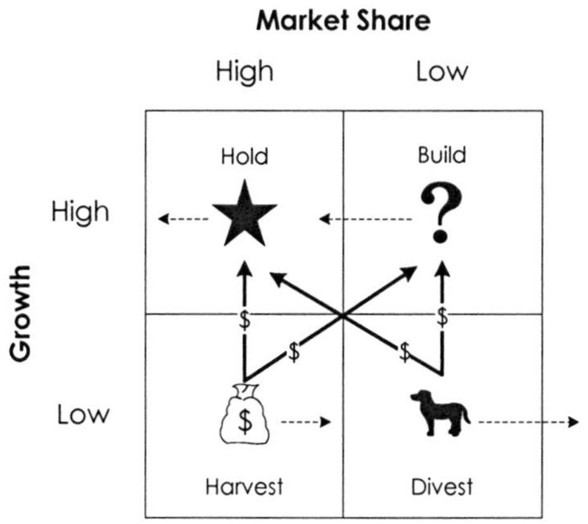

Limitations: The BCG model has numerous limitations. First, its main objective is to guide a company's resource allocation across different SBUs; as a result, it is not designed to assist with strategic decisions of a single SBU. Second, it considers market share and market growth to be the only relevant cash-allocation factors (factors such as cost, competitive reaction, synergies between SBUs, and various macroeconomic factors are not part of the model). Third, it assumes that higher market share means higher cash-generating ability and higher profitability due to economies of scale, learning curve/experience effects, monopoly power, etc., even though these factors may not apply to all industries. Fourth, market share and market growth are ambiguous and difficult to quantify. To illustrate, the same SBU can be classified as a question mark, a star, a cash cow, or a dog when alternative operational definitions of the matrix dimensions are involved. Finally, the use of the BCG matrix can have important self-fulfilling organizational implications: Labeling an SBU as a dog will lead to minimizing the cash allocated to this unit, which is likely to decrease its performance and turn the unit into a real "dog."

Application: The BCG model offers a simple strategy for evaluating the relative performance of a company's strategic business units and making cash-allocation recommendations. Its recommendations, however, are based on highly restrictive assumptions (e.g., market share and industry growth rate are the only relevant performance factors), and its application is subject to multiple interpretations (e.g., defining the industry in which the firm competes). While the general idea – classifying a company's strategic business units based on their relative performance and the attractiveness of the industry in which they compete – is a viable approach, the use of the BCG model in its original form in today's business world is rather limited.

Notes

[1] Ohmae, Kenichi (1982), *The Mind of the Strategist: The Art of Japanese Business*. New York, NY: McGraw-Hill.

[2] Asher, Mark and Eric Chung (2002), *Vault Guide to the Case Interview*. New York, NY: Vault Inc.

[3] McCarthy, E. Jerome and William D. Perreault (1996), *Basic Marketing: A Managerial Approach* (12th ed.). Homewood, IL: Irwin.

[4] Ansoff, H. Igor (1979), *Strategic Management*. New York, NY: Wiley.

[5] Adapted from Ibid.

[6] Porter, Michael E. (1979), "How Competitive Forces Shape Strategy," *Harvard Business Review*, 57, 137-145.

[7] Adapted from Ibid.

[8] Porter, Michael E. (1985), *Competitive Advantage: Creating and Sustaining Superior Performance*. New York, NY: Free Press.

[9] Adapted from Ibid.

[10] Pascale, Richard T. and Anthony G. Athos (1981), *The Art of Japanese Management: Applications for American Executives*. New York, NY: Simon and Schuster.

[11] Peters, Thomas J. and Robert H. Waterman (1982), *In Search of Excellence: Lessons from America's Best-Run Companies*. Cambridge: Harper & Row.

[12] Adapted from Ibid.

[13] Stern, Carl W. and George Stalk (1998), *Perspectives on Strategy: From the Boston Consulting Group*. New York, NY: Wiley.

[14] Adapted from Ibid.

[15] Adapted from Ibid.